CAMBRIDGE

T0245528

American EMPOWER

WORKBOOK
WITH ANSWERS

B2
UPPER INTERMEDIATE

Wayne Rimmer

CONTENTS

Contents

1A SHE IS AN INSPIRING WOMAN

1 GRAMMAR Review of tenses

a Underline the correct words to complete the text.

The other day, I was walking down the street when I ¹*have seen / was seeing / saw* Sam Carter, you know, the famous movie director. I was really excited because he ²*has been / is / was* one of my favorite directors for years, and I watch his movies all the time. "What ³*is he doing / does he do / has he done* here?" I thought to myself. There was only one way to find out. Sam ⁴*went / was going / has gone* into a café, but I stopped him before he went inside and said, "Hi, Sam!" He smiled at me, and we started to talk outside. I couldn't believe I ⁵*was talking / talked / am talking* to Sam Carter! He always ⁶*is looking / looks / has looked* so serious in photos, but he's a really friendly guy. In the end, Sam ⁷*invites / has invited / invited* me for coffee. Then he told me why he was in town. His company ⁸*made / has made / was making* a new movie with a lot of new faces in it, just ordinary people, but they needed some more.

"How about you?" Sam asked. "⁹*Did you watch / Have you watched / Are you watching* any of my movies? Do you want to be in one?" I was so shocked, I ¹⁰*have dropped / was dropping / dropped* my cup and the hot coffee went all over Sam; he yelled and ran outside. I made a terrible first impression!

b ▶ `01.01` Listen and check.

c Complete the sentences with the correct forms of the verbs in the box: simple present, present continuous, present perfect, simple past, past continuous, or past perfect.

> come   do   not finish   get   not have
> meet   remember   produce   ~~work~~   write

1 John __is working__ at a small marketing agency at the moment.
2 _____ you ever _____ anybody famous?
3 **A** What _____ you _____?
   B I'm a student.
4 Shakespeare _____ plays and poetry, and thousands of words in English come from them.
5 Our friends _____ for dinner, but they had to cancel because they were sick.
6 Not many people _____ her well now.
7 He was rich and famous, but he _____ many friends.
8 The game _____ yet; there are five minutes to go.
9 Things _____ slowly _____ worse at the office now that Mrs. Andrews has retired.
10 Eva was very happy with the design samples he _____ .

2 VOCABULARY Character adjectives

a Underline the correct words to complete the sentences.

1 Don't be so *motivated / stubborn / ambitious*! You know what I am saying makes sense.
2 I wanted him to help me, but he was very *unsympathetic / inspiring / passionate* and didn't want to do anything.
3 Margarita is a really *inspiring / sensitive / arrogant* woman and an example to everyone.
4 Nicole is *motivated / optimistic / passionate* about basketball and trains every day.
5 He's rude and *sensitive / determined / arrogant* – he thinks he's better than everyone else.
6 If you are *motivated / self-confident / pessimistic*, you do things because you really want to do them.

b Complete the crossword puzzle.

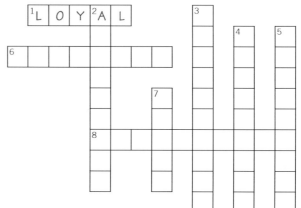

→ **Across**
1 showing firm friendship or support
6 not listening to people's opinions or changing your mind
8 thinking about the future in a positive way
↓ **Down**
2 wanting to be successful
3 making a decision and not letting anyone stop you
4 easy to hurt or upset
5 people have a good opinion of you
7 having no experience and expecting things to be all right

3 PRONUNCIATION Sound and spelling: *e*

a How is the underlined letter *e* pronounced in each word in the box? Complete the chart with the words.

> ~~conc**e**rned~~   d**e**sert   d**e**sire   d**e**ssert   h**e**lpful   id**e**ntity
> pref**e**r   priz**e**s   r**e**vise   s**e**nsitive   s**e**rvice   sl**e**pt

Sound 1 /ɪ/ (e.g., *d**e**termined*)	Sound 2 /e/ (e.g., *resp**e**cted*)	Sound 3 /ɜ/ (e.g., *s**e**rve*)
		concerned

b ▶ `01.02` Listen and check.

1B | ARE YOU FINDING IT DIFFICULT?

1 GRAMMAR Questions

a <u>Underline</u> the correct words to complete the conversation.

FABIO Hi, Gabriela. ¹*You have* / <u>*Do you have*</u> five minutes?

GABRIELA Sure. ²*What* / *What did* you want to talk to me about?

FABIO Well, I'm doing a triathlon next month. ³*Didn't* / *Weren't* you read my post?

GABRIELA No, I haven't seen it. A triathlon, wow! ⁴*What for?* / *For what?* That sounds really tough!

FABIO Yeah, it's not easy. It's swimming, biking, then running.

GABRIELA ⁵*What* / *Which* of those is the most difficult?

FABIO All of them! Um, ⁶*weren't* / *didn't* you a good swimmer once?

GABRIELA Yeah, once. What are you looking at me like ⁷*that for* / *for that*?

FABIO Do you think ⁸*could you* / *you could* coach me?

GABRIELA I don't know ⁹*if* / *what* I have enough time. ¹⁰*Can* / *Should* I think about it and call you later?

FABIO No problem. That's great! I'll swim a lot faster with your help.

GABRIELA Who ¹¹*knows* / *does know*? You might win!

b ▶ 01.03 Listen and check.

c Put the words in the correct order to make questions.

1 a / want / do / marathon / to / you / run ?
   <u>Do you want to run a marathon?</u>

2 to / this / going / is / do / why / she ?
   _____

3 the / register / who / competition / need to / for / doesn't ?
   _____

4 giving / why / our / aren't / tickets / they / us ?
   _____

5 of / which / to do / would you / the challenges / like ?
   _____

6 have / the most / ever done / you / difficult / what is / thing ?
   _____

7 for / did / hard training / what / this / we do / all ?
   _____

8 the / happened / of / what / at / end / the game ?
   _____

9 have / think we / of / a chance / you / do / winning ?
   _____

10 your / who / website / designed ?
   _____

2 VOCABULARY Trying and succeeding

a Complete the sentences with the phrases in the box. There is one extra phrase you do not need.

succeed in   give up   stick with   keep it up
manage to   try out   ~~work out~~

1 Sandra likes to <u>work out</u> at the gym on her lunch break.

2 José wants to _____ a new recipe for lemon cake.

3 We really need to _____ fast food.

4 Charlie told his kids to _____.

5 The Smiths didn't _____ assemble their kitchen table.

6 It won't be easy to _____ this diet.

b Complete the sentences with the phrases in the box.

give up   ~~take a chance~~   stick with   keep it up
make an effort   manage to   drop out   try out   work out

1 I'd like to *take a chance* at snowboarding, but I'm afraid of falling and breaking something.

2 If you _____ of this class, you won't graduate on time with all of us.

3 If you _____ this training program, you'll get back in shape.

4 I play tennis on Saturdays, and I also _____ once or twice a week at the gym.

5 My car is at the mechanic's, and I don't know if they'll _____ repair it by Monday.

6 Ben went sailing with me twice and he's terrible at it, but he doesn't want to _____.

7 Your writing has improved a lot this semester, so _____.

8 Would you like to _____ the new version of the software?

9 I know Jade's not interested in the project, but she could at least _____ to get involved.

1C EVERYDAY ENGLISH
Don't touch the food

1 CONVERSATION SKILLS
Cutting a conversation short

a Check (✓) the best way to cut the conversation short.

1 Sorry, but _____ now.
   a ✓ I really have to go
   b ☐ I have to finish
   c ☐ there's nothing else to say

2 _____ Speak to you soon.
   a ☐ I have nothing else to say.
   b ☐ Are we finished?
   c ☐ Got to run now.

3 OK, _____.
   a ☐ I look forward to speaking to you
   b ☐ see you tomorrow
   c ☐ that's enough

4 _____, Irena.
   a ☐ Talk to you later
   b ☐ Tell me again
   c ☐ We'll speak about this

5 _____ Can you call later?
   a ☐ This is not convenient.
   b ☐ Who's speaking?
   c ☐ Can't talk now.

6 Well, I have to _____.
   a ☐ leave
   b ☐ run
   c ☐ end

7 Bye, nice _____.
   a ☐ conversation
   b ☐ talking to you
   c ☐ day

8 I have no time _____ now, but thanks for calling.
   a ☐ to run
   b ☐ talking
   c ☐ to talk

2 USEFUL LANGUAGE
Explaining and checking understanding

a Put the excerpts in the correct order to explain how to take a good photo.

☐ Always remember to keep still. If the camera moves, you get a bad photo.

☐ Is that clear? Do you want me to explain any of this again?

☐ But whatever camera you buy, read the instructions carefully. Make sure you know what your camera can do. Did you get that?

1 You don't need to get a very expensive camera. These have a lot of functions you just don't need. Do you know what I mean?

☐ Another thing to remember is to take your time. Only real professionals can take good photos in a hurry.

☐ When you take a photo, the most important thing is the light. Basically, the more light, the better, so choose the right time of day and place. Do you get the idea?

b ▶ 01.04 Listen and check.

3 PRONUNCIATION Rapid speech

a ▶ 01.05 Listen. Check (✓) the sentences where you hear the final /t/ of the underlined words.

1 ☐ I <u>must</u> go and see her soon.
2 ☐ The nurse said I <u>must</u> eat less bread.
3 ☐ We've <u>got</u> to have more help.
4 ☐ Sorry, you <u>can't</u> take one with you.
5 ☐ <u>Haven't</u> any of the people arrived?
6 ☐ Sarah said she <u>didn't</u> do the homework.
7 ☐ Claudia has been there, <u>hasn't</u> she?
8 ☐ The store <u>might</u> open again.
9 ☐ We <u>can't</u> use our phones here.
10 ☐ The children <u>must</u> go first.

1D SKILLS FOR WRITING
I really missed my phone all day

Face-to-Face Texting

1 READING

a Read the article. Are the sentences true or false?

1 The woman has the same opinion as most other people.
2 She has noticed an imbalance in communication.
3 The experiment involved the couple not communicating for a day.
4 It was a positive experience for them.
5 Technology has made us forget our priorities.
6 We don't need technology.

b Read the article again and check (✓) the best ending for the sentences.

1 The purpose of the first paragraph is … .
   a ✓ to explain the writer's motivation
   b ☐ to compare different types of communication
   c ☐ to introduce a theory about communication

2 The main rule of the experiment was that they … .
   a ☐ had to communicate as little as possible
   b ☐ couldn't say anything to each other
   c ☐ needed to explain things very simply

3 The point about breakfast is that … .
   a ☐ making meals involves technology
   b ☐ it was an amusing situation
   c ☐ everything was so simple

4 The rest of the day showed that the experiment … .
   a ☐ needed to continue for longer
   b ☐ only worked until a friend got involved
   c ☐ was not as easy as they thought

5 She texted her husband to discuss … .
   a ☐ plans for a party
   b ☐ the effectiveness of the experiment
   c ☐ her friend's communication problems

6 The conclusion is that … .
   a ☐ the experiment was mostly a failure
   b ☐ technology has changed relationships between people
   c ☐ speaking is still an effective kind of communication

2 WRITING SKILLS
Organizing an article

a Read the tips (1–8) for writing an article.
Is the advice good or bad? Check (✓) the correct box.

When you're writing an article, …	Good	Bad
1 plan the structure of your article before you start writing it.	✓	
2 write the article in your own language first, then translate it.		
3 write short paragraphs with one or two sentences.		
4 include questions to engage the reader.		
5 use a dictionary to find interesting words and phrases.		
6 use linking words and expressions to join ideas.		
7 evaluate ideas – write what you think about them.		
8 check your writing when you have finished.		

A lot of people think that technology brings people closer together, but I'm not so sure. People spend so much time texting and looking at screens that they hardly ever speak to one another. This made me think, and I decided to do a little experiment.

One day my husband and I decided not to speak to each other at all. We could email, text, etc., but we couldn't actually communicate in spoken words. So, at breakfast, he sent me a text asking if I wanted any more toast, and I replied that I didn't, but I wouldn't mind another cup of coffee.

We both thought it was funny at first, but things got more complicated as the day went on. For example, a friend called me about a special party she was organizing. I had to text my husband for about 20 minutes to discuss everything.

The whole thing made me appreciate that nothing can replace face-to-face communication – talking to each other. Communication may be easier because of technology, but people aren't machines. We sometimes forget that simple things are often the most important in life.

3 WRITING

a Imagine that for one week you had to walk or bike to get around instead of using a car or public transportation. Write an article about your experience. Use the notes and your own ideas to help you.

> Introduction: how you usually get around, your feelings about walking / biking vs. cars / public transportation
>
> Your experience: good things (exercise, see interesting things, cheaper)
>
> Your experience: difficulties (takes longer, bad weather, dangerous?)
>
> Evaluation: walking / biking better in some situations, should use cars / public transportation less

1 READING

a Read the article and check (✓) the statement that matches Nick's attitude about his own body.

1 ☐ It's more difficult living without arms and legs now than when he was younger.
2 ☐ His physical condition means he is generally worried about trying new things.
3 ☐ He gets on with his life, even though he has no arms or legs.

> **Have you ever thought about what it might be like to live just a single day without being able to use your hands or legs? This is everyday life for Nick Vujicic, who was born without any limbs. However, Nick doesn't let his condition stop him – he regularly takes part in sports, he has traveled all over the world, and he's also happily married with a young child. And unlike many able-bodied people, he can even swim and surf.**

Before Nick Vujicic was born, his parents had no idea that he would go on to have any medical problems – none of the medical checkups had shown a problem. However, when he was born, it was clear that his life would be different from that of other babies. Growing up would not be easy. His parents decided to send him to a neighborhood school, where he would use a wheelchair, and where there were people available to assist him. The experience was difficult, but Nick feels it was the best decision his parents could have made because it gave him a sense of independence. Unsurprisingly, when he was in school, he sometimes felt depressed and lonely and was sometimes bullied. But he always had the support of his loyal friends and family, and these people made him determined to overcome many problems. He even went on to study at a university, where he earned a degree in financial planning and real estate.

What surprises many people is just how optimistic Nick can be and how many different things he has managed to do. Much of this is because of his parents. His father put him in the water for the first time when he was 18 months so that Nick would be self-confident enough to swim when he was older. He has one small foot which he can use to help him move around in the water. He is able to operate a computer by using the toe on this foot to type, something he learned to do when he was just six years old. And when he plays golf – yes, he even plays golf – he is able to hold the golf club under his chin.

A big part of Nick's life now is giving motivational talks. He travels around the world and has shared his inspiring story with millions of people, speaking to audiences in packed stadiums. Nick's message is that you should never give up and that people should love themselves even when they fail.

b Read the article again and check (✓) the correct answers.

1 Nick's parents knew he would be born without arms and legs.
  a ☐ true   b ☑ false   c ☐ doesn't say

2 Nick was sometimes unhappy when he was in school.
  a ☐ true   b ☐ false   c ☐ doesn't say

3 Nick could swim when he was just 18 months old.
  a ☐ true   b ☐ false   c ☐ doesn't say

4 Nick uses a mouse to operate a computer.
  a ☐ true   b ☐ false   c ☐ doesn't say

5 Nick uses the toe on his foot to play a sport.
  a ☐ true   b ☐ false   c ☐ doesn't say

6 The stadiums where Nick speaks are full.
  a ☐ true   b ☐ false   c ☐ doesn't say

c Write a paragraph about an outstanding person you know or have heard about who has helped others. Remember to include:

• what the person does and why you are impressed by this
• any difficulties the person has had in their life
• how the person has helped other people.

2 LISTENING

a ▶ 01.06 Listen to Michael and Sarah talking about Frane Selak, who some people have called the unluckiest man in the world. Put the events in the order they happened.

- [ ] a plane crash
- [ ] a bus crash
- [ ] winning the lottery
- [1] a train crash
- [ ] a car accident
- [ ] being hit by a bus
- [ ] a car falling off a mountain

b Listen again and Check (✓) the correct answers.

1 What happened to Selak when he was in the train crash?
- a [ ] He was very seriously injured.
- b [✓] He had an injury.
- c [ ] He wasn't injured.

2 What is true about the plane crash that Selak survived?
- a [ ] Several other people also survived the crash.
- b [ ] He escaped through a door after it crashed.
- c [ ] He was helped by a problem with the plane.

3 What was the cause of the bus crash?
- a [ ] the weather
- b [ ] the speed of the bus
- c [ ] a technical problem with the bus

4 What is true about the first incident with a car that Selak had?
- a [ ] He was not driving the car when it developed a problem.
- b [ ] The car exploded just after he got out.
- c [ ] Flames came into the car from the engine while he was driving it.

5 Why did his car go off the side of the mountain in the later accident?
- a [ ] He was hit by a truck.
- b [ ] He hit a tree and lost control.
- c [ ] He had to change direction to avoid a truck.

6 Which of the following sentences is true about when Selak won the lottery?
- a [ ] He often played the lottery at that time.
- b [ ] He occasionally played the lottery at that time.
- c [ ] He had never played the lottery before.

7 What is Sarah's opinion of Selak's story?
- a [ ] She is sure it's true.
- b [ ] She is not sure if it's true.
- c [ ] She is sure it's untrue.

8 What does Michael say about Selak?
- a [ ] He thinks that Selak is probably telling the truth.
- b [ ] He thinks that Selak shouldn't invent stories.
- c [ ] He thinks it's strange that Selak gave away his lottery winnings.

c Write about a time when you were very lucky or unlucky. Use these questions to help you:
- What was the situation? What were you doing?
- Why were you lucky or unlucky?
- How did you feel?
- Was anybody else with you? How did he or she feel?
- Do you think this happens to a lot of people?

👁 Review and extension

1 GRAMMAR

Check (✓) the correct sentences. Correct the wrong sentences.

1 [ ] I write this letter to complain about the service.
   I am writing this letter to complain about the service.
2 [ ] Take any train. They all go there.
3 [ ] She lived in that town since she was a child.
4 [ ] Have you ever heard from her again afterward?
5 [ ] I was taking a shower when the water turned cold.
6 [ ] I don't know Tom. How is he?
7 [ ] Why you didn't tell me?
8 [ ] What is the currency in Thailand?

2 VOCABULARY

Check (✓) the correct sentences. Correct the wrong sentences.

1 [ ] There are determined subjects everyone should study.
   There are certain subjects everyone should study.
2 [ ] Don't mention it to Laura. She's pretty sensible about it.
3 [ ] The mayor is very respective in this town.
4 [ ] The president gave a passionated speech about crime.
5 [ ] I'd love to take a chance at diving.
6 [ ] I have a plan, and I'm going to stick with it.

3 WORDPOWER *make*

Match sentences 1–7 with responses a–g.

1 [a] Should we go by car or walk?
2 [ ] Why is it taking him such a long time to decide?
3 [ ] I'm really afraid of your dog.
4 [ ] Can't you just follow the instructions?
5 [ ] How can I stay in a place like this?
6 [ ] Can you read that sign?
7 [ ] What are the flowers for?

a It makes no difference to me.
b He can never make up his mind.
c It's only trying to make friends.
d Just make the best of it.
e They don't make any sense.
f I want to make up for being late.
g No, I can't make out what it says.

2A | IT WAS GETTING LATE AND I WAS LOST

1 GRAMMAR Narrative tenses

a Underline the correct words to complete the sentences.

1 I _took_ / _was taking_ / _had taken_ a quick shower and ran for the bus.
2 Sorry, when you called, I _spoke_ / _was speaking_ / _had spoken_ to a customer.
3 By the time Megan arrived for dinner, everyone _left_ / _had left_ / _has left_.
4 He _set_ / _had set_ / _was setting_ the watch to 00:00 and began to run the marathon.
5 The phone _had been_ / _was_ / _has been_ ringing for about a minute when I answered it.
6 What _have you done_ / _had you done_ / _were you doing_ in the garage all that time?
7 We _were buying_ / _bought_ / _had been buying_ some fruit and went to the next store.
8 Someone _had broken_ / _was breaking_ / _had been breaking_ the window, but we didn't see who it was.
9 Hi, _had you waited_ / _were you waiting_ / _you waited_ for me?
10 The manager stood up and _had given_ / _was giving_ / _gave_ a speech.

b Complete the text with the correct forms of the words in parentheses.

One evening many years ago, I ¹ _was thinking_ (think) about what to do when my friend Maria called. Maria was in a good mood because she ² _____ (finish) all her exams and was free now. She ³ _____ (come) over, and we decided to go for a walk. We ⁴ _____ (go) very far when we saw something very unusual inside the old building near the market. Years earlier, the place ⁵ _____ (burn) down. No one knew how the fire ⁶ _____ (start), but ever since then, the place had been empty. Anyway, in one of the windows we saw a face, the face of a young girl. She obviously ⁷ _____ (cry) because there were still tears on her face. It ⁸ _____ (get) dark by then, but we could still see her clearly. "⁹ _____ (you / see) that?" I whispered to Maria. We ¹⁰ _____ (never / be) in this building before and felt a little scared, but we ¹¹ _____ (go) inside to find the girl. She ¹² _____ (wear) some really old clothes. They were dirty and smelled of smoke. "I ¹³ _____ (get) out," she said, crying again. "I was too late!" We looked at each other and ¹⁴ _____ (run) all the way home. The place is now a restaurant, and all our friends wonder why Maria and I will never go there with them!

c ▶02.01 Listen and check.

2 VOCABULARY Expressions with _get_

a Complete the sentences with the words in the box.

| attention | away | ~~down~~ | hold | involved | point | rid | swept |

1 All this gray weather is really getting me ___down___, and I feel depressed.
2 There isn't enough space. We need to get _____ of all this trash.
3 I tried to get _____ of the balloon, but I couldn't and it floated away.
4 The waves are really big, so be careful not to get _____ away.
5 Let's get straight to the _____ and not waste time.
6 To get the server's _____ in this restaurant, you need to ring the bell.
7 It's been a very long semester. I'd like to get _____ this summer – not sure where.
8 Don't get _____ in all of Karen's problems. People will start blaming you.

b Complete the sentences under the pictures with the expressions in the box.

| get through | ~~get to~~ | get into trouble | get anywhere |
| get the feeling | get on my nerves |

1 I had fun with my brother. I hope I'll _get to_ play with him again soon.
2 I'm not sure I'll _____ all this today.
3 I _____ this will be over quickly.
4 The company won't _____ with this new product.
5 He might _____ going to school like that.
6 All this crying is starting to _____.

3 PRONUNCIATION _had been_

a ▶02.02 Listen to the sentences and check (✓) the ones that include _had_.

Sentence 1	✓	Sentence 6	☐
Sentence 2	☐	Sentence 7	☐
Sentence 3	☐	Sentence 8	☐
Sentence 4	☐	Sentence 9	☐
Sentence 5	☐	Sentence 10	☐

2B IF IT RUNS TOWARD YOU, DON'T RUN AWAY

1 GRAMMAR
Future time clauses and conditionals

a Underline the correct words to complete the conversation.

MARIO Hi, Silvia. Are you coming camping with us?
SILVIA [1]*If / When* you still want me to, sure.
MARIO Great. It should be a lot of fun [2]*if / unless* the weather gets bad.
SILVIA [3]*As long as / If* we get a couple of days of decent weather, I don't mind. What do I need to take?
MARIO The usual stuff. [4]*When / If* I get home, I'll text you the list I've made just in case. You don't need to worry about food, though. I've packed enough [5]*in case / provided* you like pasta. That's the easiest thing to make.
SILVIA Fine. [6]*If / In case* we run out of pasta, I'll take some canned tuna and rice.
MARIO Good idea. [7]*If / Provided* you want, bring some cards. We could play at night.
SILVIA Sure. That'll be fun [8]*when / as long as* I don't forget to pack them. Text me tomorrow [9]*as long as / as soon as* you get up.
MARIO OK. Remember to buy pepper spray because we might see bears.
SILVIA [10]*If / Unless* I see a bear, I'll run all the way home!

b ▶ 02.03 Listen and check.

c Match 1–8 with a–h to make sentences.
1. [b] Call your mom
2. [ ] It's perfectly safe
3. [ ] I like to go for a swim
4. [ ] It's ideal for a vacation
5. [ ] Take some sunscreen
6. [ ] I'll go on the trip
7. [ ] Don't go
8. [ ] You can go any time

a provided you like somewhere quiet.
b when you get there.
c unless you do something stupid.
d as long as you do.
e provided you tell me first.
f in case you need it.
g if you don't want to.
h if it's really warm.

2 VOCABULARY
Animals and the environment

a Find eight words about animals that match these clues.
1. a set of similar animals or plants
2. a living thing that is not a plant
3. the natural surroundings where we live
4. the place where an animal or plant naturally lives or grows
5. kept safe by laws that prevent people from harming them
6. animals or plants that could disappear without our help
7. uncommon and difficult to find
8. catch and kill animals for food or sport

A	E	N	V	I	R	O	N	M	E	N	T	E	U	L
K	N	C	R	H	B	E	X	U	D	D	O	X	K	E
X	D	T	S	G	T	I	C	U	L	E	T	C	E	L
S	A	D	S	N	P	C	L	N	Y	P	B	E	K	M
U	N	Q	E	T	B	S	R	I	A	R	N	P	Y	J
C	G	L	M	R	A	M	A	O	T	O	T	T	X	K
O	E	X	T	T	S	N	R	O	R	T	A	I	J	Z
C	R	E	A	T	U	R	E	Q	K	E	G	O	S	L
S	E	B	R	I	L	L	I	A	N	C	L	N	H	B
F	D	K	I	H	L	E	D	G	N	T	D	A	P	L
U	F	L	A	U	C	C	N	S	P	E	C	I	E	S
L	P	J	H	N	F	Y	Q	T	D	D	G	A	S	R
B	U	V	J	T	J	Z	Q	K	E	I	B	B	B	C
Y	Z	Z	I	I	R	M	P	H	A	B	I	T	A	T
S	K	T	S	X	A	Z	D	I	J	G	B	W	D	X

b Complete the text with the words in the box.

risk ~~creatures~~ environment extinct
natural hunt survive kill

Look at this photo of a group of lions. This might be a very rare sight in the future. Lions are beautiful [1] *creatures* , but they are very much at [2]_____ in the modern world. The European lion has been [3]_____ for 2,000 years, and now lions only [4]_____ in India and parts of Africa. People still [5]_____ lions and [6]_____ them, and our damage to the [7]_____ is making it difficult for lions to find places to live and feed. We can help by protecting lions' [8]_____ habitat, which is the African savannah and the forests of Gujarat in India.

1 CONVERSATION SKILLS
Agreeing using question tags

a Complete the question tags in the conversations with the words in the box.

aren't could did don't haven't isn't do wasn't

MIKE It's a beautiful day!

LUCY It's great, [1]_____isn't_____ it? Why don't we go to the beach?

MIKE Yes, let's go!

LUCY We could drive but let's walk. We need the exercise.

MIKE We do, [2]_____ we? I'll get my things.

LUCY Last time you forgot your towel.

MIKE That's right. I didn't have it with me, [3]_____ I? Now I remember that I borrowed yours. Anyway, let's go.

Later ...

LUCY That was great, [4]_____ it? I'm really hungry now.

MIKE Me too. This place looks good.

LUCY Yeah, we've been here before, [5]_____ we? They make really good pizza.

MIKE That's right. Oh, I don't have my wallet. You couldn't lend me some money, [6]_____ you?

LUCY First a towel, then your wallet. You never remember anything, [7]_____ you?

MIKE Well, we're friends, [8]_____ we? Come on, let's go inside.

b ▶️02.04 Listen and check.

2 USEFUL LANGUAGE
Giving compliments and responding

a Check (✓) the best response for the sentences.

1 You're so good about recycling.
   a ✓ Do you think so?
   b ☐ What do you think?
   c ☐ I'm glad you like it.

2 Your hair is amazing!
   a ☐ You're welcome.
   b ☐ I'm glad you like it.
   c ☐ I think so.

3 You really managed to get it just right.
   a ☐ Guess it's not bad.
   b ☐ Yes, I managed it.
   c ☐ Didn't I?

4 The color is just perfect.
   a ☐ Yes, it is.
   b ☐ It's not bad, is it?
   c ☐ That's right, isn't it?

5 It's so tasty!
   a ☐ It's all right.
   b ☐ Not at all.
   c ☐ That's great.

6 That was a wonderful present!
   a ☐ The same to you.
   b ☐ Yes, it was.
   c ☐ I'm glad you like it.

b ▶️02.05 Listen and check.

3 PRONUNCIATION
Intonation in question tags

a ▶️02.06 Listen to the intonation in the questions. Is the speaker asking a real question or just checking information? Check (✓) the correct box.

		Asking a question	Checking information
1	It was a great idea, wasn't it?		✓
2	You don't know where Tustin Avenue is, do you?		
3	That's obvious, isn't it?		
4	They just didn't understand, did they?		
5	He hasn't finished college yet, has he?		
6	I'm not on the team, am I?		
7	They will be able to do it, won't they?		
8	You've been there before, haven't you?		
9	She's forgotten all about it, hasn't she?		
10	She's not going to agree, is she?		

2D | SKILLS FOR WRITING
Make sure you know where you're going

1 READING

a Read the leaflet and <u>underline</u> the best heading for each section.

b Read the leaflet again. Are the sentences true or false?

1 It's easy to find an orienteering club.
2 Everyone should do the same training.
3 You should buy some good shoes.
4 You won't need to buy a map.
5 A fast start is important.
6 You should respect the environment you run through.
7 You only need a compass if you get lost.
8 The main thing is to have fun.

2 WRITING SKILLS
Organizing guidelines in a leaflet

a Check (✓) the best introduction to a leaflet about collecting mushrooms.

a ☐ For centuries, people have collected mushrooms all over the world. The purpose of this leaflet is to discuss the reasons why mushroom picking is popular and to provide some practical suggestions to those who want to follow this tradition.

b ☐ Collecting mushrooms might seem like a strange pastime, but it's very popular in many countries, especially in Eastern Europe. You need to be careful about which mushrooms you pick, but this is a fun way of spending time.

c ☐ Why pick mushrooms? Many people think it is better to buy them from a supermarket, but there are advantages of getting them yourself provided that you don't pick the wrong ones!

d ☐ Onc day I was at home when my friend called and suggested going out to the forest and picking some mushrooms. At first, I thought it was a crazy idea, but I went anyway and actually enjoyed it. Here is my advice for people who want to do the same.

3 WRITING

a Read the plan for the rest of the leaflet. Then complete the leaflet using these headings and notes.

> **Preparation**
> 1 When? (autumn, mornings)
> 2 Where? (forests, near trees)
> 3 Need warm clothes, good shoes/boots
> 4 Check weather
>
> **In the forest**
> 5 Be careful in forest – animals, accidents
> 6 Only pick mushrooms you know (go with expert, use the Internet)
> 7 Don't get lost!
> 8 Protect environment (litter)
>
> **At home**
> 9 Eat or freeze mushrooms
> 10 Many recipes for mushrooms – soup, pies, etc.

> **Orienteering is a sport where you follow a route with a map and compass and try to get between the points as fast as possible.**

1 *Preparation / Getting Into the Sport / Advantages of Orienteering*
- Orienteering is usually organized in forests. Just search online to find a club near you.

2 *Training / Dangers of Forests / Running Fast*
- You need to be fit to run around forests. If you're lucky, you might live near a forest, but most people will need to do some running in parks or on roads.
- Unless you are very fit already, start with fast walking and then build up to running.

3 *What You Need / Expenses / Shopping for Orienteering*
- You don't need to spend a lot of money on equipment, but a good pair of shoes is essential.
- You'll get a map at the course, and you can borrow a compass as well.

4 *Win! / Be Careful! / On the Day*
- Start slowly and save your energy.
- Don't damage any plants or trees. You are only there for the day, but the forest is there forever.
- You won't get lost provided you use your compass and go in a straight line.
- Enjoy yourself!

3A I'M NOT VERY GOOD IN THE MORNING

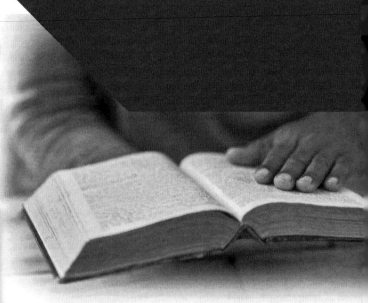

1 GRAMMAR Multi-word verbs

a Underline the correct words to complete the text.

When I was in school, I didn't think I was good at anything. The other kids picked things ¹*out / in / up* really quickly, but I didn't, and some kids looked ²*down on / on down / down* me as some kind of loser. The only thing that I was interested in was cars, and I spent hours in the garage with my mom's old car, checking ³*it out / out it / out*. My mom wasn't ⁴*at / by / into* cars at all though, and she was tired of me going ⁵*in with / on about / with* them all the time. Anyway, one day there was a school trip. I woke ⁶*by / up / on* early to catch the bus. We were going down the road when the bus suddenly stopped. I thought we had run out ⁷*in / at / of* gas, but the driver told us there was an engine problem and he would have to call a mechanic. I went to see for myself and quickly figured ⁸*out / by / through* what to do: I just needed to put a cable back. After ten minutes, the bus was on the road again. After that, everyone looked ⁹*to me up / up to me / me up to*, and I realized there was something I could do well. When I finished school, I set ¹⁰*out / up / by* my own car repair business, and now I'm doing really well.

b ▶ 03.01 Listen and check.

c Put the words in the correct order to make sentences and questions.

1 all / but / I / threw / sorry, / it / away .
   Sorry, but I threw it all away.

2 let / try / hardest and / your / us / down / don't .
   _____

3 fell / not friends / out / I / and we're / Tony / with .
   _____

4 away / you / like that / can't / get / mistakes / with .
   _____

5 yourself / for / it / and figure / go / out .
   _____

6 just / why / don't / it / you / out / try ?
   _____

7 made / Michelle / up / him / it / impress / to .
   _____

8 in / you / you're doing / what / to / believe / need .
   _____

9 up / anyone / a better / come / can / with / idea ?
   _____

10 picked / difficult, / I soon / it / but / is / French / up .
   _____

2 VOCABULARY Ability and achievement

a Underline the correct words to complete the conversation.

MARIANA Have you heard of this writer Daniel Kalder?

LIAM Yes, I read *Strange Telescopes* a while ago. It's a(n) ¹*talented / extraordinary* book.

MARIANA I agree. Kalder has this ²*ability / potential* to make a serious statement but make you laugh at the same time.

LIAM It really is ³*able / outstanding*. I just wish I had some ⁴*ability / talent* for writing.

MARIANA Kalder is ⁵*successful / talented* because he spent so many years improving his style. That kind of hard work is ⁶*successful / exceptional*.

LIAM True. I don't think many people have heard of Kalder yet, but he has the ⁷*potential / achievement* to be a really well-known writer.

MARIANA He's very ⁸*skilled / potential* at what he does, so I wish him all the best.

b ▶ 03.02 Listen and check.

c Correct the mistake in each sentence.

1 You need to have a talent to it.
   You need to have a talent for it.

2 Olympic athletes are all exceptional for their field.
   _____

3 She's really successful by what she does.
   _____

4 I became very skilled for the game.
   _____

5 The ability of running long distances is important.
   _____

6 Work hard if you want to be extraordinary on a skill.
   _____

7 He has the potential of being world champion one day.
   _____

8 Carl Lewis was outstanding for the long jump.
   _____

3B THERE ARE A LOT OF GOOD RUNNERS IN KENYA

1 GRAMMAR
Present perfect and present perfect continuous

a Underline the correct words to complete the sentences and questions.

1 *I've always loved* / *I always loved* baseball. It's my favorite sport.
2 *They've won* / *They won* the championship two years ago.
3 What *have you thought* / *did you think* of the game?
4 The players *haven't arrived* / *didn't arrive* yet, so the game can't begin.
5 *I've been running* / *I was running* in the park when it happened.
6 Marina *has been doing* / *was doing* yoga since she was a teenager.
7 I have *completed* / *been completing* five marathons.
8 **A** Why is your shirt wet?
  B *I've run* / *I've been running*.
9 Joshua hasn't *played* / *been playing* tennis since he was in college.
10 Our martial arts trainer has *learned* / *been learning* Japanese for ten years.

b Complete the text with the correct forms of the verbs in parentheses.

Shantelle Gaston-Hird [1] _has just broken_ (just / break) a world record! Yesterday in Manchester, England, she [2] _____ (run) a half-marathon – that's just over 21 kilometers – in 2 hours, 16 minutes, and 3 seconds. Shantelle is 32 years old, and this is the second time she [3] _____ (beat) all the best runners in the world. From March 2017 to January 2019, Shantelle [4] _____ (hold) the world record, and now, just ten months later, she [5] _____ (set) a new world record!

Shantelle started retro-running – running backward – for fun, but soon after, she began to take her hobby more seriously. But that's not all! She [6] _____ (also / complete) five marathons and eight ultra-marathons. It's safe to say that Shantelle [7] _____ (run) forward and backward for quite a while!

Every time she [8] _____ (race), she [9] _____ (represent) a charity. This time, Shantelle represented YoungMinds, a mental health charity for children and young people. She wants to show people that consistent training and determination can get extraordinary results.

c ▶ 03.03 Listen and check.

2 VOCABULARY
Words connected with sports

a Read the definitions and write the words.

1 the act of winning a competition   _victory_
2 a person who is in charge of a sports game   _____
3 shout approval or encouragement   _____
4 people who watch a sports event   _____
5 be in a competition for your country   _____
6 an area for playing sports, especially soccer   _____

b Complete the text with the correct forms of the words in parentheses.

Everyone thinks that [1] _professional_ (profession) athletes get paid a lot of money to [2] _____ (competitor), but this is not always true. The top [3] _____ (athletics) in smaller sports like handball, mountain running, and women's volleyball don't earn much money. Such sports are very [4] _____ (competition), and the athletes [5] _____ (training) hard, but even if they [6] _____ (representation) their country, they often can't make a living from their sport. Unfortunately, [7] _____ (victor) in [8] _____ (champion) and new world [9] _____ (recording) very often don't mean money, especially if the sport isn't popular on TV. But maybe this doesn't matter if the athletes enjoy what they do and spectators are happy to watch them perform and [10] _____ (cheerful) for them. Money isn't everything, after all.

c ▶ 03.04 Listen and check.

3 PRONUNCIATION Word stress

a ▶ 03.05 Listen to the conversation and underline the stressed syllables in the highlighted words.

ELENA I know you like track and field, but do you ever take part in [1]competitions?

DAVID Sometimes – in fact, I'm going to [2]compete in the national [3]championships next weekend.

ELENA So you're almost a [4]professional [5]athlete then?

DAVID Not really. It's hardly a [6]profession, but I do a lot of [7]training, and I'm hoping for a good [8]performance. There'll be a lot of strong [9]competitors, and I'll have to [10]perform really well on the big day.

ELENA So [11]victory might be yours then, and we'll welcome the [12]victorious champion home?

DAVID Don't laugh, I might win!

3C EVERYDAY ENGLISH
Who should we invite?

1 USEFUL LANGUAGE Making careful suggestions; Keeping to the topic of the conversation

a Put the words in the correct order to make sentences and questions.

1 could / go / swimming / we / day / always / another .
   We could always go swimming another day.

2 thing / price / remember / another / to / is the .
   _____

3 stay / maybe / I / should / home / think / we .
   _____

4 idea / ask / think / to / a / don't you / it's / good ?
   _____

5 how / sound / we watch / does / on Sunday / a / movie / if / it ?
   _____

6 to / that / but / easier / it'd / eat out / agree / be / don't you ?
   _____

b Correct the mistake in each sentence.

1 Don't you think it's a good idea take some food?
   Don't you think it's a good idea to take some food?

2 Anyway, as I was speaking, Tessa needs to decide.
   _____

3 Another idea might be for going the day before.
   _____

4 Just going to what I was saying before.
   _____

5 I thought maybe we could to invite Simon.
   _____

6 Of course, we could always checking online.
   _____

7 But don't you agree that it's be better to ask first?
   _____

8 So, to get back at Martin and his problems.
   _____

2 PRONUNCIATION Consonant sounds

a Decide if the <u>underlined</u> letters have a voiced sound or unvoiced sound. Write *V* (voiced) or *U* (unvoiced).

1	<u>g</u>ame	V	<u>c</u>ame	U	6	sa<u>v</u>e		safe	
2	<u>b</u>each		<u>p</u>each		7	<u>p</u>ie		<u>b</u>uy	
3	<u>f</u>erry		<u>v</u>ery		8	<u>p</u>ig		<u>p</u>ick	
4	sim<u>p</u>le		sym<u>b</u>ol		9	<u>p</u>ack		<u>b</u>ack	
5	<u>g</u>irl		<u>c</u>url		10	ha<u>v</u>e a		ha<u>v</u>e to	

b ▶ 03.06 Listen and check.

3D SKILLS FOR WRITING
It doesn't matter what sport people choose

1 READING

a Look at the bar chart and read the article. Match paragraphs 1–5 with their functions a–e.

a ☐ It adds extra information not shown in the data.
b ☐ It interprets the data in more detail.
c ☐ It states some additional things to consider about the data and the future.
d ☑ 1 It outlines the issue that the data tries to answer.
e ☐ It explains what the bar chart is about.

b Look at the bar chart and read the article again. Check (✓) the correct answers.

1 The chart includes 13-year-olds from Puerto Rico.
  a ☐ true   b ☐ false   c ☑ doesn't say

2 Each category is very specific.
  a ☐ true   b ☐ false   c ☐ doesn't say

3 Older teenagers are doing more homework.
  a ☐ true   b ☐ false   c ☐ doesn't say

4 There is no great change between the figures for sports.
  a ☐ true   b ☐ false   c ☐ doesn't say

5 There are no major patterns in the data.
  a ☐ true   b ☐ false   c ☐ doesn't say

6 The article ends with a reference to the future.
  a ☐ true   b ☐ false   c ☐ doesn't say

2 WRITING SKILLS Describing data

a Look at the bar chart below that compares sports fans by generation across different sports in the U.S. Then complete the sentences with the numbers and words in the box. There are two extra ones you do not need.

| 16   5   3   20   decrease   increase   least   most |

1 Only about ____5____ % of millennials are big fans of soccer.

2 However, the percentage of loyal basketball fans has remained the same at _____ %.

3 The _____ popular sport in the U.S. is American football.

4 There has been a slight _____ of loyal sports fans in most sports.

5 There has been about a _____ % drop in hockey fans from the previous generation.

6 About _____ % of Generation X closely watch baseball in the U.S.

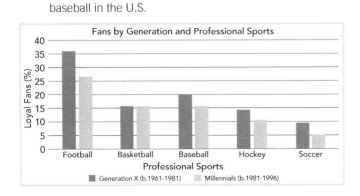

Fans by Generation and Professional Sports
■ Generation X (b.1961-1981) ■ Millennials (b.1981-1996)

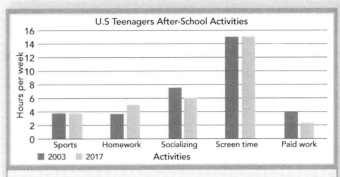

U.S Teenagers After-School Activities
■ 2003 ■ 2017

1 School is a big part of teenagers' lives, but there are many ways they spend the rest of their time. Are teenagers basically the same these days, or are their needs and interests changing?

2 The bar chart looks at five different categories of activities that teenagers do after school. It is quantified in hours per school week, so hours from Monday to Friday. Some categories have stayed very similar across the years, but others have changed considerably.

3 It's important to note that the categories are very broad. Screen time, for example, can include gaming, going online, watching TV, and watching videos.

4 The most noticeable changes have occurred in the categories of homework, socializing, and paid work. Teenagers appear to be spending less time at paid jobs and in social situations, but they're doing homework more than ever.

5 It is important to remember that these are not the only ways teenagers spend their time. For example, the chart doesn't mention eating or sleeping. Do you think teenagers sleep less now than they did in the past? The world has changed a lot over the past 20 years, so it will be interesting to see what the future brings.

3 WRITING

a Look at the bar chart in 2a again. Then write an article about how millennials follow sports today. Use the notes to help you.

- more options – sports fans now follow more sports but watch fewer complete games
- different priorities – people have shorter attention spans
- TV – not so popular today; time may be inconvenient
- Internet – apps and social media provide instant access and news all the time
- lifestyle – single millennials without kids spend less time at home

Reading and listening extension

1 READING

a Read the article about one of the greatest runners of all time. Check (✓) the statements that are true.

1 ☐ Johnson's running style was considered strange.
2 ☐ Johnson had the potential to win more than he did.
3 ☐ Johnson loved the attention he got from his success.
4 ☐ Johnson had a different style from Usain Bolt.

b Read the article again and check (✓) the correct answers.

1 The fact that Michael Johnson's friends laughed at his running style made him want to run even faster.
  a ☐ true   c ✓ doesn't say
  b ☐ false

2 It was considered surprising that Johnson was able to win both the 200 and 400 meters.
  a ☐ true   c ☐ doesn't say
  b ☐ false

3 Johnson was the first person to win the 400 meters at one Olympic Games and then win it again in the following Olympic Games.
  a ☐ true   c ☐ doesn't say
  b ☐ false

4 Johnson was injured during the 1988 Olympic Games.
  a ☐ true   c ☐ doesn't say
  b ☐ false

5 Johnson didn't race in the 200 meters final at the Barcelona Olympics.
  a ☐ true   c ☐ doesn't say
  b ☐ false

6 Johnson often refused to speak to journalists when he was very famous.
  a ☐ true   c ☐ doesn't say
  b ☐ false

7 Johnson now says that he might have been more successful if he'd been as relaxed as Usain Bolt.
  a ☐ true   c ☐ doesn't say
  b ☐ false

8 Usain Bolt is currently trying to beat Johnson's 400-meter world record.
  a ☐ true   c ☐ doesn't say
  b ☐ false

c Write a paragraph about someone who has achieved a lot. Remember to include:

- some basic information about the person
- what they achieved and how they achieved it
- what other people think of them.

MICHAEL JOHNSON
THE MAN IN THE GOLDEN SHOES

Michael Johnson is one of the most successful professional athletes of all time. He won four Olympic gold medals and eight World Championship golds. People used to think that it was impossible for the same person to win the 200 meters as well as the 400 meters, but Johnson won both at the 1996 Atlanta Olympics, setting a new world record for both – 19.32 seconds and 43.49 seconds. He then went on to win the 400 meters again in Sydney in 2000 – the first time anyone had ever won the race in two Olympic Games in a row.

Anyone who saw Johnson perform in a race – even on TV – will remember him. He was an outstanding athlete, of course, but he also had a very unusual running style – short steps and a very straight back. When he was a child, his friends used to laugh at him because of how he ran. They said it was funny. Johnson later said he'd found it funny, too, but for another reason – the style was helping him win all his races.

Many people think that with better luck, Johnson might have won even more medals – he was expected to be part of the team that went to the 1988 Olympics, but he had an injury and wasn't selected. Then in 1992, he got sick after eating in a restaurant two weeks before the start of the Barcelona Olympics. As a result, he didn't get as far as the final that he had been expected to win. In 1996, he avoided bad luck and the success story began.

Johnson's success made him rich and famous, and he was one of track and field's first "superstars" – well known to the general public around the world, not just to sports fans. But he didn't always seem to enjoy the fame – he sometimes sounded bad-tempered in interviews and, with the golden shoes that he started to wear when racing, some called him arrogant. After retiring, he explained that he'd found the press attention annoying.

Johnson, of course, had a natural talent for running, but many people say that it was his ability to focus and his dedication to training that made him so exceptional. The big running star of today – Usain Bolt – is famously relaxed, almost the opposite of Johnson. Whether Johnson could have run faster if he'd taken Bolt's more relaxed approach is up for debate – Johnson has said he certainly doesn't think so.

Johnson has since lost his 200-meter world record to Bolt and has encouraged him to try the 400 meters as well, even though this might mean Johnson could lose his world record. One thing is for sure – it would be fascinating to know who would win a race between Bolt and Johnson at his best.

Review and extension

1 GRAMMAR

Check (✓) the correct sentences. Correct the wrong sentences.

1. ☐ The police are trying to check who stole the money.
   The police are trying to find out who stole the money.
2. ☐ He's too young. He's still growing up.
3. ☐ It's warm. Put your sweater off.
4. ☐ We're finding a new secretary right now.
5. ☐ What ideas have you come up with?
6. ☐ Monica wasn't told about it yet.
7. ☐ Don't worry. I already sent the letter.
8. ☐ I'm waiting for you for a long time!
9. ☐ I'm sure you've heard of Bigfoot.
10. ☐ I don't know. I didn't decide yet.

2 LISTENING

a ▶ 03.07 Listen to a conversation between two friends about their school days. Match names 1–5 with a–e to make sentences.

1. ☐ Julia   a argued with Mark.
2. ☐ Martina   b believed in Mark.
3. ☐ Mr. Edwards   c was good at math.
4. ☐ Sarah   d was good at sports.
5. ☐ Mrs. Taylor   e was good at teaching grammar.

b Listen again. Look at the opinions. Who has these opinions – Tina, Mark, or both? Check (✓) the correct box.

		Tina	Mark	Both Mark and Tina
1	Martina is likely to have a successful career now.			✓
2	Julia was very arrogant.			
3	Mr. Edwards was a very good teacher.			
4	Sarah didn't have a good relationship with anybody at the school.			
5	Learning French at school wasn't very enjoyable.			
6	The school trips were not always educational.			

c Write a conversation between two people discussing their school days. Person A tells Person B about a subject they were good at. Person B tells Person A about a subject they were bad at. Use these questions to help you:

• Why was Person A good at their school subject?
• Was Person A naturally good at the school subject, or did they have to study hard?
• Why was Person B bad at their school subject?
• Is Person B good at this school subject now?

2 VOCABULARY

Check (✓) the correct sentences. Correct the wrong sentences.

1. ☐ What are the secrets of success people?
   What are the secrets of successful people?
2. ☐ It's not able to get there by public transportation.
3. ☐ No one doubts her capacity to get to the very top.
4. ☐ It was another fantastic performance by the Kenyan.
5. ☐ There is a training course for all new staff tomorrow.
6. ☐ Professional sports are very competitive.
7. ☐ What did the spectators think of the movie?
8. ☐ The soccer players are just coming out on the court.

3 WORDPOWER *up*

Read the sentences. Write *up* in the correct places.

1. We came early, but Greg turned late.
   We came early, but Greg turned up late.
2. If you don't know it, look it online.
3. She thought about it and decided not to bring the topic.
4. I used it all yesterday, so I went and bought some more.
5. We looked at the check and added it again.
6. I went running with Percem, but I couldn't keep with her.
7. I started to learn Spanish and picked it pretty quickly.
8. He works so hard; I've always looked to him.

⟳ REVIEW YOUR PROGRESS

Look again at Review Your Progress on p. 42 of the Student's Book. How well can you do these things now?
3 = very well   2 = well   1 = not so well

I CAN ...	
discuss ability and achievement	☐
discuss sports activities and issues	☐
make careful suggestions	☐
write a description of data.	☐

4A | SHE'S HAPPIER NOW THAN SHE USED TO BE

1 GRAMMAR used to and would

a <u>Underline</u> the correct words to complete the sentences.

1 Yesterday my boss *used to come* / <u>*came*</u> to work late.
2 People *used to* / *would* believe the sun went around the Earth.
3 One hundred years ago, it *couldn't* / *wouldn't* snow at all in winter.
4 We *lived* / *would live* in a small town before we moved to Toronto.
5 I *would* / *used to* have a car, but I sold it.
6 That really *wasn't* / *didn't use to be* the best decision.
7 Julia *is used to working* / *used to work* in a store before she started her own business.
8 Sam *got used to* / *used to* sharing an apartment when he was a college student.
9 I *wasn't used to* / *got used to* getting up so early, so the first morning was a shock.
10 It took me a long time to *be* / *get* used to wearing a uniform at work.

b ▶ 04.01 <u>Underline</u> the correct words to complete the text. Then listen and check.

> Richard Morgan lives on a boat in Chesapeake Bay in Virginia. His life ¹*would* / *used to* / *was used to* be very different a few months ago. Richard ²*graduated* / *used to graduate* / *would graduate* from law school in 2010 and got a great job at a law firm. It was interesting and paid well, but it was a very difficult job. Richard ³*was used to* / *got used to* / *used to* work 12–14 hours a day, and sometimes he ⁴*would sleep* / *was used to sleeping* / *got used to sleeping* at the office because it was so late. Richard ⁵*used to realize* / *would realize* / *realized* that this kind of life was killing him. "I ⁶*was used to* / *used to* / *would* spending all my time at work. It was normal for me – that was the frightening thing," Richard says.
>
> On Sundays, Richard ⁷*used to going* / *got used to go* / *would go* for a walk along the bay, and he always enjoyed this. So one day, when he had had enough, he ⁸*decided* / *used to decide* / *was used to deciding* to change his life completely. He gave up his job, bought a boat, and said goodbye to his stressful life as a lawyer. "It was a big change. I still haven't ⁹*used to* / *gotten used to* / *been used to* the ducks waking me up, but it's a great life," he says. "My family and friends were shocked at first, but now they ¹⁰*get used to visiting* / *are used to visiting* / *used to visiting* me on my boat, and they know I'm happy."

2 VOCABULARY Cause and result

a Correct the mistake in each sentence.

1 Smoking can lead in a lot of health problems.
   <u>Smoking can lead to a lot of health problems.</u>

2 No one knows what the affect was.
   _____

3 That's the main cause for the problem.
   _____

4 It could effect millions of people.
   _____

5 As a result from this, there is less money to spend.
   _____

6 The new law resulted of protests and demonstrations.
   _____

7 Generally, it's had a positive effect in people.
   _____

b Complete the text with the words in the box.

> affect   as a result   ~~cause~~   effect
> is caused by   lead   result

> What makes people unhappy? Some people think that the biggest ¹ <u>cause</u> is stress, whether from work or the pressures of life. Lifestyle certainly has a heavy influence on happiness. For example, a poor diet can ² _____ your health and ³ _____ in illness and disease. Some people also think that unhappiness ⁴ _____ loneliness. Friends do have a positive ⁵ _____ on people's lives because friends provide support, entertainment, and company. It's more complicated with family because relationships are often difficult and ⁶ _____ can ⁷ _____ to conflict and stress. This is clearly a difficult question to answer.

4B | WE WEREN'T ALLOWED TO TALK IN CLASS

1 GRAMMAR Modality review; Obligation and permission

a Complete the conversation with the responses in the box.

> I had to catch the 5:30 train.
> I'm tired during the day.
> No, I can work from home on Fridays.
> No, I don't have to unless we have a deadline.
> ~~No, I had to get up at 5:00 this morning.~~
> Yes, I can find a seat on the train.
> Yes, the boss lets us stay at home one day.
> You should speak to my boss!

JANE Are you feeling all right?
ALEX [1] No, I had to get up at 5:00 this morning.
JANE What for?
ALEX [2] _____
JANE Do you do this every morning?
ALEX [3] _____
JANE Is that the same for everyone?
ALEX [4] _____
JANE Are there any advantages of getting to work early?
ALEX [5] _____
JANE And the disadvantages?
ALEX [6] _____
JANE Do you need to work late as well?
ALEX [7] _____
JANE You need to ask for a raise.
ALEX [8] _____

b Underline the correct words to complete the sentences.

1 It's for girls only, so he *can / can't / has to* take part in the competition.
2 You really *can / ought to / don't have to* read this book about Jackie Chan. It's great.
3 Lola *mustn't / doesn't have to / shouldn't* train hard because she is very talented.
4 You *shouldn't / don't have to / are not allowed to* get nervous before the race.
5 The competition *was supposed / had / ought* to start at 7:00, but everyone was late.
6 Don't worry, you *must not / shouldn't / don't need to* train today.
7 My trainer made me *run / to run / running* ten kilometers.
8 During training, we're not allowed *eat / to eat / eating* certain food.
9 Don't let them *beat / to beat / beating* you in the race!
10 They were *let / allowed to / forced to* train in the cold and rain, even though they didn't want to.

2 VOCABULARY Talking about difficulty

a Underline the correct adjectives for the pictures.

1 a(n) *arduous / strict* journey
2 *tricky / rigorous* testing
3 *testing / strict* discipline

4 a(n) *tricky / exhausting* training schedule
5 *tough / punishing* standards
6 a *tricky / grueling* situation

b Underline the correct words to complete the conversation.

KATE So what's it like to be a firefighter, Marco?
MARCO It's really [1]*straightforward / strict / tough*, much harder than I thought. The training is very [2]*rigorous / awkward / delicate*, and the instructors really [3]*struggle / stretch / demand* us.
KATE But you've finished all the training?
MARCO Not yet. It's not so [4]*strict / demanding / straightforward* to become a firefighter. First, there's this [5]*arduous / straightforward / delicate* training schedule and then a [6]*grueling / tricky / backbreaking* written test at the end.
KATE Well, you do like a [7]*struggle / punishment / challenge*! It sounds like a very [8]*rigorous / demanding / tricky* job.

c ▶ 04.02 Listen and check.

3 PRONUNCIATION
Sound and spelling: *u*

a ▶ 04.03 Listen to the words in the box. How is the underlined letter *u* pronounced in each word? Complete the chart with the words.

> ~~umbrella~~   p<u>u</u>ll   <u>u</u>seless   s<u>u</u>gar   s<u>u</u>pper
> attit<u>u</u>de   res<u>u</u>lt   infl<u>u</u>ential   enth<u>u</u>siasm

Sound 1 /ʌ/ (e.g., *cup*)	Sound 2 /ʊ/ (e.g., *cook*)	Sound 3 /u/ or /ju/ (e.g., *food* or *cube*)
umbrella		

4C EVERYDAY ENGLISH
They're not *that* boring

1 CONVERSATION SKILLS
Expressing careful disagreement

a Complete the chart with the phrases in the box.

> I don't agree with you.
> Really, do you think so?
> That's just not true.
> Oh, I don't know.
> Maybe you're right, but …
> You can't really believe that.
> I know what you mean, but on the other hand …
> No way!
> I'm not sure about that.
> I'm afraid you're wrong there.

Careful disagreement	Direct disagreement
	I don't agree with you.

b Complete the conversation with the sentences in the box.

> I know what you mean, but on the other hand, technology is so important.
> Really, do you think so?
> I'm not sure about that. They work very hard.
> Oh, I don't know. Some things are improving.
> Maybe you're right, but teachers are not the real problem.

BETO Education is getting worse and worse in this country.

LILY ¹*Oh, I don't know. Some things are improving.*

BETO Like what? Teachers don't know what they're doing.

LILY ² _____

BETO Yes, but they need more training.

LILY ³ _____

BETO True – kids just don't want to study.

LILY ⁴ _____

BETO I do. They spend way too much time playing on their phones.

LILY ⁵ _____

BETO Hang on, someone's texting me …

c ▶ 04.04 Listen and check.

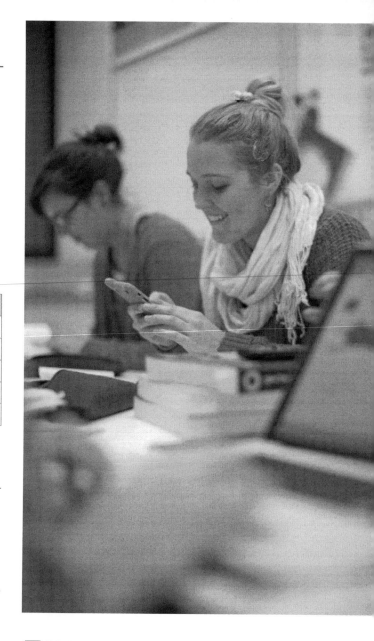

2 PRONUNCIATION Contrastive stress

a ▶ 04.05 Listen to the exchanges. <u>Underline</u> the word in each response with the strongest stress.

1 **A** It was an absolutely terrible hotel! I never want to go there again.
   B Oh, I don't know. It wasn't that bad.
2 **A** I really didn't like that movie. It was so boring!
   B Oh, I don't know. It wasn't that boring.
3 **A** I loved that restaurant. The menu was really original.
   B Oh, I don't know. It wasn't that original.
4 **A** Have you seen that new store? It looks great!
   B Oh, I don't know. It doesn't look that great.
5 **A** I thought the meeting today was way too long.
   B Oh, I don't know. It wasn't that long.

4D SKILLS FOR WRITING
I'm good at communicating with people

> Do you want to learn new skills and live and work in a beautiful environment? Volunteer to work as a forest ranger in a variety of locations with Forest Conservation Alliance.
>
> **RESPONSIBILITIES**
> You will carry out work around the forest, protect the environment, and provide help to visitors and the general public.
>
> What we offer you
> * free accommodation
> * training and education
> * the opportunity to learn new skills
>
> **QUALIFICATIONS**
> You care about the environment and are a good team worker.
> You have a basic knowledge of a subject related to the environment.
> You have good oral and written communication skills in English.

✉ ✎ ☆ ⚑   ⊗

Re: Volunteers

Dear Forest Conservation Alliance,

I saw the ad for volunteers to work as forest rangers, and I would like to apply.

I am a student of environmental science in Rio de Janeiro, and I have traveled to the U.S. many times, so my language skills are very strong. I am also a friendly and sociable person who enjoys working with people.

As a student, I am in an excellent position to explain the beauty of the forest to visitors and to protect the forest from damage. I strongly believe that forests are essential for the world to survive, and it is the work of rangers to make people aware of this.

In our studies, we have field trips to forests to study their natural beauty. I also spend a lot of my free time outdoors exploring. I am sure this knowledge and enthusiasm would help me in this position.

I am confident that I can be an important part of your team. I am reliable and hardworking, so this challenge is ideal for me. When I finish college, I would like to work in this field, so this is a wonderful opportunity.

I look forward to hearing from you.

Best regards,

Carla Nazario

---

1 READING

a Read the job ad and Carla's email. Then complete the summary with the words in the box.

> fluently   forests   outside   people
> ~~ranger~~   reliable   strong   student

Carla wants to apply for a job as a ¹___ranger___. She is a ²_____ and speaks English ³_____. Carla loves spending time ⁴_____ in ⁵_____ and other interesting places. She likes to work with ⁶_____ and describes herself as ⁷_____. Carla sounds like a ⁸_____ candidate.

b Read the ad and the email again. Are the sentences true or false?

1 There are several places to work.
2 You don't need to find somewhere to live.
3 Carla has only been to the U.S. once.
4 She has finished her studies.
5 Carla thinks that the world will not survive without forests.
6 She has some practical experience.
7 Carla is worried about the responsibility.
8 In the future, she wants to be a ranger.

2 WRITING SKILLS
Giving a positive impression

a Add the correct missing word to each sentence.

1 I would ___like___ to apply to be a volunteer at the Winter Olympics.
2 I have always been interested _____ sports.
3 I would be more than happy to _____ up my free time.
4 I am in an excellent _____ to help athletes and visitors.
5 I _____ believe that sports bring people together.
6 I look _____ to hearing from you.

3 WRITING

a Read the ad and the plan. Then write an application email.

> **Do you want to be part of an international team and support the world's greatest sporting event? Become a volunteer at the Winter Olympics with Olympics United!**
>
> **Responsibilities**
> There are a range of opportunities depending on your experience and skills, such as preparing food for athletes, helping in the medical center, and interpreting.
>
> What we offer you
> * free accommodation
> * tickets to events
> * the opportunity to learn new skills
>
> **Qualifications**
> You are physically fit.
>
> You have good oral and written communication skills in English.
>
> ✉ Apply for this job
>
> ☆ Save to favorites

> **Plan**
>
> Paragraph 1: reason for writing
> Paragraph 2: your background (work / education), your communication skills
> Paragraph 3: your experience, personality, and other skills, how these make you a good candidate
> Paragraph 4: why you want to be a volunteer, your interest in sports / the Olympics
> Paragraph 5: closing sentence

BLOG

Train Travel and Unwritten Rules
[posted by Paul, yesterday at 7:14 p.m.]

Well, I've just arrived home furious! Why? Something pretty silly, really, but very annoying. As most of you reading probably know, I commute to work every day by train. Today, I was standing with a few other people by the train doors as the train pulled into the station. Now, what's supposed to happen is that people get off the train first, and then the people who are on the platform get on. It works better that way. It's the logical way to do it. But today, as soon as the doors opened, everyone on the platform started to get on, and we had to kind of fight our way off. There was no advantage for the people on the platform to get on the train first – they still had to wait for everyone else to get off, and it just created confusion, although I suppose they were worried about finding a seat on the train. While it was all happening, I got angry and ended up having an argument with someone getting on.

Anyway, it got me thinking. There's no rule anywhere that says that the people on the platform are supposed to wait and let the people on the train get off first. That's just what people do. It's an unwritten rule. So, what other unwritten rules can you think of? Do you ever see people breaking them? And if so, what do you do?

COMMENTS

Sam: yesterday at 7:43 p.m.
Exactly the same problem on the bus recently. Everyone tries to get on without letting anyone off first! It doesn't make sense – what's the hurry?

Irene: yesterday at 11:11 p.m.
Another unwritten rule? Waiting in line! There are some places, like clothing stores, where there are actually barriers that make you form a line, but generally we just do it without thinking. And if someone cuts in line? Generally I say nothing – at most I tend to give them a dirty look, but that's a waste of time because they're already in front of me in the line and can't see my face!

Sara: today at 9:11 a.m.
I suppose politely holding a door open for someone is another unwritten rule. It's funny because I think sometimes it would be easier for everyone not to – if the other person isn't directly behind you, you have to wait for them, and also they have to hurry so you're not waiting too long! But I always do it. If someone doesn't hold the door open for me, then I think they're rude.

Juan: today at 11:15 a.m.
Tipping is an unwritten rule, but I find that the rule changes a lot depending on the country! I grew up in a country where you'd only leave money if you thought the server was really good or you had a great time. But here in the U.S., everyone leaves 18%, even if the service isn't that good. I prefer the unwritten rule in my country!

1 READING

a Read the blog post and comments. Check (✓) the things that are not mentioned by the writer or in the comments.

1 ☐ Behavior on public transportation
2 ☐ Waiting in lines
3 ☐ Doing something to be polite
4 ☐ Regretting doing something rude
5 ☐ Paying extra for something

b Read the blog and comments again. Write the names of the people.

1 Which person mentions something they do that is pointless? _____
2 Which person compares a situation in two different countries? _____
3 Which person cannot understand a particular behavior of other people? _____
4 Which person describes a polite form of behavior that may have a negative result? _____
5 Which person suggests they may understand why rude behavior took place? _____

c Read the blog and comments again. Are the sentences true or false?

1 The original writer, Paul, was involved in a violent situation.
2 Paul believes there needs to be a written rule to tell people to wait before getting on the train.
3 Irene doesn't normally argue with people who cut in line.
4 Sara doesn't expect people to hold the door open for her.
5 Juan doesn't agree with tipping practices in the U.S.

d Write a paragraph about an "unwritten rule" in your country or a country you know well. You should say:

• what the rule is
• whether you think the rule is necessary
• what you or other people tend to do when the rule is broken.

2 LISTENING

a ▶ **04.06** Listen to some interviews with college graduates. How many are unhappy with their final grades at university? Check (✓) the correct answer.

1 ☐ one student   3 ☐ three students
2 ☐ two students   4 ☐ all four students

b Listen again and check (✓) the correct answers.

1 What do we learn about Mateo's year?
   a ☐ He studied a lot during this period.
   b ☐ He had to buy a lot of books.
   c ☐ He was very busy at work.

2 Why did Mateo find his experience at university difficult?
   a ☐ He had to pay a lot for his studies.
   b ☐ He has a young family to look after.
   c ☐ He had to work and study at the same time.

3 Why did Samantha mention that she had three exams in two days?
   a ☐ to show that this was really the only difficulty she had
   b ☐ because she is unhappy with the university administration
   c ☐ to explain how little control you have over your schedule as a student

4 Why didn't Luke get the final grade he wanted?
   a ☐ He had a bad cold during the last two exams.
   b ☐ His performance on his final two exams wasn't strong enough.
   c ☐ He was really sick on the day of one exam.

5 Which of the following opinions does Luke express?
   a ☐ He doesn't think that you should have to take an exam if you are really sick.
   b ☐ He is sure he would have gotten the grade he wanted if he hadn't been sick.
   c ☐ He thinks the university shouldn't consider illness only on the day of an exam.

6 Which of the following statements best matches something Jane says?
   a ☐ You need to get a lot of sleep to succeed in college.
   b ☐ It's harder to get a degree if you don't have friends or family who have gone to college.
   c ☐ It's better to go to college before you're 40.

7 What do we learn about Jane's work situation?
   a ☐ She hopes she will get a chance to advance more at work now that she's graduated.
   b ☐ She's found a new job since she graduated.
   c ☐ She thinks it's going to be hard to find a job even though she now has a college degree.

c Write about an event that has had a big influence on your life. Use these questions to help you:

- What was the event?
- Why was it important for you?
- What was your life like before the event?
- How did your life change after the event?

◉ Review and extension

1 GRAMMAR

Check (✓) the correct sentences. Correct the wrong sentences.

1 ☐ My grandpa use to work in a factory near Detroit.
   My grandpa used to work in a factory near Detroit.
2 ☐ I would prefer to see my own doctor.
3 ☐ She used to living by herself now.
4 ☐ This can be the last time we come here.
5 ☐ I hope we could do this again some time.
6 ☐ If you want to apply, you should fill out this form.

2 VOCABULARY

Check (✓) the correct sentences. Correct the wrong sentences.

1 ☐ Sunday is better cause I'm free then.
   Sunday is better because I'm free then.
2 ☐ I'm worried that it might effect my health.
3 ☐ It can lead to all kinds of problems.
4 ☐ My first teacher was very strickt.
5 ☐ She left because she felt she needed a new challenge.
6 ☐ Prisons are basically for punish criminals.

3 WORDPOWER *as*

Underline the correct words to complete the sentences.

1 The rules of the game are as *follows* / *a whole* – first, there must be at least five players.
2 It looks as *a matter of fact* / *if* we were all wrong.
3 There's a lot to do there as *far as* / *for* entertainment is concerned.
4 The competition was good for the country as *a whole* / *follows* – everyone benefitted.
5 She's still on vacation as far as *I'm concerned* / *I know*.
6 The tickets are too expensive and as far as *I'm concerned* / *I know*, they're a waste of money.
7 More people live in the U.K. than in Spain. As *a whole* / *a matter of fact*, the population is almost 67 million.
8 Alice is very nice, but as *for* / *if* her husband – well, he's kind of strange.

⟳ REVIEW YOUR PROGRESS

Look again at Review Your Progress on p. 54 of the Student's Book. How well can you do these things now?
3 = very well   2 = well   1 = not so well

I CAN ...	
discuss events that changed my life	☐
discuss and describe rules	☐
describe photos	☐
write an email to apply for work.	☐

5A | YOU COULD LIVE TO BE A HUNDRED

1 GRAMMAR Future probability

a Underline the correct words to complete the conversation.

KATY Have you read this article, Josh? It says there's a good [1]*chance / doubt* the next generation will live to be 150 years old!

JOSH Who knows, what it says [2]*may / will* be true. But what evidence is there?

KATY Advances in medicine [3]*might / will* certainly be a factor, and people [4]*won't / couldn't* die from all kinds of diseases common today. Also, technology [5]*will probably / probably will* make everyday life easier.

JOSH Fine, but I [6]*don't think / doubt* if many people will want to live that long. It's [7]*unlikely / sure* that it'll be much fun to be 150.

KATY The article says that we [8]*may / will* probably be able to work until that age. There's a good chance [9]*of / that* machines [10]*will / won't* do all the hard work, such as washing and cleaning, so that we can do different tasks, such as critical thinking.

JOSH Interesting. I'm [11]*probable / sure* there'll even be a special Olympics for people over 100!

KATY Yes, it's bound [12]*to happen / happen*, so start training!

b ▶05.01 Listen and check.

c Check (✓) the correct words to complete the sentences.

1 Pollution _____ be even worse in the future if we don't start taking responsibility for it.
   a ✓ will probably b ☐ probably will c ☐ likely will

2 I'm sure that it _____ happen in our lifetime.
   a ☐ may not b ☐ might not c ☐ won't

3 Virtual reality _____ become more popular, but I doubt it.
   a ☐ might b ☐ will c ☐ can

4 The question is _____ we find a real solution to our energy problems?
   a ☐ may b ☐ might c ☐ will

5 Movie theaters _____ go out of business in the future.
   a ☐ likely will c ☐ won't likely
   b ☐ will likely

6 It's unlikely _____ computers will replace teachers.
   a ☐ for b ☐ if c ☐ that

7 There's no _____ that they will stop printing books.
   a ☐ likely b ☐ probability c ☐ chance

8 I can't _____ that one day we will be able to choose the sex of our babies.
   a ☐ imagine b ☐ suppose c ☐ guess

9 Airport security is sure _____ change with new technology.
   a ☐ to b ☐ that c ☐ of

10 Productivity at work is _____ to get better soon now that we can work from home.
   a ☐ possible b ☐ bound c ☐ probable

2 VOCABULARY
Adjectives describing attitude

a Complete the words.

1 How r <u>e a l i s t i</u> c is it that we'll live to 150 years old? I mean will it actually happen?

2 Sam is always late handing in work. He's completely u_ r _ _ _ _ b _e.

3 It was an u _ _ y _ _ _ _ _ e _ _ c comment, and he immediately felt sorry he'd said it.

4 Victoria is really a_ v _ _ _ _ r _ _ s. She just went on a trekking vacation in the Ecuadorian rainforest.

5 Wendy is really t _ _ _ _ _ _ f _ _, so she will always check on you when you're sick or upset about something.

6 You can tell he's w_ _l o _ _ _ _ _z _ d by looking at how clean his desk is.

b Complete the sentences with the words in the box. There are four extra words you do not need.

adventurous   ambitious   cautious   ~~critical~~
disorganized   irresponsible   reliable   thoughtful
uncompetitive   unrealistic   unsympathetic

1 He's very _critical_ of the way the work was done.

2 I've never known anyone so _____; you can never count on him.

3 It's dangerous out there; I guess it's better to be _____ and play it safe.

4 Even if the place is a little _____, we still know where everything is.

5 I may be _____ compared to everyone else, but I still want to win.

6 That was a really _____ trip – you won't believe all the incredible things that happened.

7 The new server is obviously very _____. I've never seen anyone work as hard as him.

3 PRONUNCIATION Sound and spelling: *th*

a How are the <u>underlined</u> letters *th* pronounced in each word in the box? Complete the chart with the words.

<u>th</u>letic   brea<u>th</u>   brea<u>th</u>ing   mo<u>th</u>er   Ear<u>th</u>   ei<u>th</u>er
lea<u>th</u>er   leng<u>th</u>   mon<u>th</u>   <u>th</u>e   ~~<u>th</u>ink~~   <u>th</u>ough

Sound 1 /θ/ (e.g., *th*ank)	Sound 2 /ð/ (e.g., *th*en)
think	

b ▶05.02 Listen and check.

28

5B I'LL BE SETTLING INTO MY ACCOMMODATIONS

1 GRAMMAR Future perfect and future continuous

a Underline the correct words to complete the sentences.

1 Passengers, we will soon *be arriving* / *have arrived* at the station.
2 You can still help because they won't *have finished* / *be finishing* yet.
3 Will polar bears still *be living* / *have lived* in the Arctic 50 years from now?
4 We'll *be feeding* / *have fed* the penguins at 2:30, so make sure you see that.
5 The team will *have completed* / *be completing* their project by 2031.
6 What will we *be achieving* / *have achieved* after we've spent all this money on research?
7 I don't think we'll *have driven* / *be driving* cars in 20 years' time.
8 Camilla will *be learning* / *have learned* a lot by the time she leaves Antarctica.
9 This time tomorrow, I'll *be getting* / *have gotten* ready to go.
10 Camilla will be glad to get back because she won't *be seeing* / *have seen* her friends for a long time.

b Complete the text with the future continuous or future perfect forms of the verbs in the box.

change   complain   not cook   create   destroy
not eat   not fall   go   not live   replace   study
transport   turn   walk

Let's travel to the year 2059! We ¹won't be living on Earth because pollution and wars ²_____ the old planet. Instead, planet Zeus will be our home. Giant spaceships ³_____ everyone and everything from Earth before it exploded in 2055. Zeus won't be a bad place to live, and some things will go on as normal. Adults ⁴_____ to work every morning. Children ⁵_____ in school, and old people ⁶_____ about almost everything. Many things will be different, though. Because of the different atmosphere, our hair ⁷_____ green – at least it ⁸_____ out – and we ⁹_____ around in space suits. Special pills ¹⁰_____ food and drink, so we ¹¹_____ at all, and we ¹²_____ out at restaurants. Yes, life ¹³_____ a lot. Welcome to 2059, and the future we ¹⁴_____.

c ▶ 05.03 Listen and check.

2 VOCABULARY The natural world

a Match 1–7 with a–g to make sentences.

1 [e] Big companies don't seem to worry enough about the ecological
2 [ ] There was a period of rough
3 [ ] There are people who think that climate
4 [ ] We make an effort to be environmentally
5 [ ] Just look at the river to see the effect of global
6 [ ] We don't realize that we live in a fragile
7 [ ] I read that solar

a change is some kind of myth.
b energy is one of the fastest growing forms of energy.
c environment and everything is interconnected.
d friendly, but it's not always easy.
e impact of what they do.
f warming on water levels.
g weather, and we couldn't go out much.

b Complete the words.

1 Global w.arming is changing animals' natural habitats.
2 Cities are trying to be more environmentally f_____.
3 Obviously, s_____ energy is a cleaner alternative than oil and gas.

4 Tourism can damage the desert's fragile e_____.
5 We can reduce our carbon f_____ by taking fewer flights.
6 It would be crazy to go out to sea in this r_____ weather.

7 Recent winters have been colder as a result of c_____ change.
8 Just stop and think about the ecological i_____ of how we live.

5C EVERYDAY ENGLISH
I'm not making enough money

1 USEFUL LANGUAGE Discussing advantages and disadvantages

a <u>Underline</u> the correct words to complete the conversation.

MAGDA You know, I'm seriously thinking [1]*at / of / on* taking this job in Paris.

PABLO You should! One good [2]*thing / advantage / problem* is the higher salary. It's basically a promotion.

MAGDA True, but the trouble [3]*by / for / with* that is more pressure and stress. A big disadvantage [4]*by / of / for* the position I've been offered is that I'll have too much to do.

PABLO Come on, one of the best things [5]*about / with / of* you is how you respond to a challenge.

MAGDA I guess so ... Another problem [6]*at / from / with* this job offer is that I'll need to improve my French – and fast!

PABLO No need to worry [7]*for / at / about* that either. The advantage [8]*for / of / at* living and working in a foreign country is that you learn the language quickly.

MAGDA You have an answer for everything!

PABLO The only drawback [9]*of / by / in* the job I can see is the size of the company. Do you really want to work in a company that big?

MAGDA If they pay me enough money, yes!

b ▶ 05.04 Listen and check.

2 CONVERSATION SKILLS Responding to an idea

a Complete the conversation with the responses in the box.

> That's a great idea! I can't remember the last time you made one.
> That's a possibility, although we might have to invite them in for coffee or something.
> Hmm, I don't know about that. I'm not in the mood for spicy food.
> That's not a bad idea. They'd need to drive there, though.
> Yes, that makes sense. I need the exercise!
> ~~It's an idea, I suppose. Where should we go?~~
> That might be worth a try, and it's not far.

A How about eating out tonight for a change?
B [1]<u>It's an idea, I suppose. Where should we go?</u>
A There's a new Thai place that just opened.
B [2]_____
A Well, there's the Italian place just up the hill.
B [3]_____
A Let's walk there. It's a beautiful day.
B [4]_____
A We could invite Amelia and Rob, too.
B [5]_____
A Then they could give us a ride if we feel too lazy to walk back.
B [6]_____
A So I have an excuse to make one of your favorite lemon cakes.
B [7]_____

b ▶ 05.05 Listen and check.

3 PRONUNCIATION Intonation groups

a ▶ 05.06 Listen and <u>underline</u> the words that are stressed in the sentences.

1 The <u>trouble</u> <u>is</u> it could take a long time to get the money.
2 The good thing is we're not far from downtown.
3 The problem is people are starting to talk about her.
4 The advantage is the price isn't very high.
5 The drawback is no one really knows what's going to happen.
6 The advantage is we can see a lot more of each other.
7 The trouble is I'm not sure I have time to help him.
8 A disadvantage is it means selling the car.

5D SKILLS FOR WRITING
We need to change the way we live

1 READING

a Read the essay and complete the summary with the words in the box.

> against   conclusion   crisis   ~~essay~~
> for   growth   manage

This ¹____essay____ discusses whether population
²_____ is a problem. It considers arguments first
³_____ and then ⁴_____ the idea and comes
to the ⁵_____ that there won't be any major
⁶_____ if we ⁷_____ resources properly.

b Read the essay again. Are the sentences true or false?

1 Population growth is a new concern.
2 Food prices are rising.
3 The shortage of water is causing climate change.
4 There are ways of turning seawater into drinking water.
5 The real issue is how we share food and water.
6 The population will eventually stop growing.

2 WRITING SKILLS Arguing for and against an idea

a Are the arguments for or against giving aid to developing countries? Check (✓) the correct box.

	For	Against
1 Some of the aid is lost and stolen.		✓
2 Wealth needs to be shared around the world.		
3 We have a moral responsibility to help people in need.		
4 Giving aid makes developing countries dependent.		
5 We have problems to worry about in our own country.		
6 Developing countries could become important markets or partners.		
7 It will mean fewer problems with illegal immigration.		
8 There are always rich and poor countries – that's just how things are.		

People have always worried about population growth. It is a fact that the number of people on the planet is increasing very quickly, in some countries more than others. This puts a lot of pressure on Earth's resources. But is population growth really leading to some kind of crisis?

Many people believe that we just cannot produce enough food to feed everyone. The increase in food prices is proof of this. Furthermore, clean drinking water is getting harder to find, a situation made worse by climate change.

However, not everyone agrees with these arguments. We could produce food much more efficiently with technology, and in the same way we could treat seawater to produce an almost endless supply of drinking water. Some people point out that our problem is distribution of resources, and this is something we can solve.

Overall, population growth is a concern, but there should be enough food and water for everyone if we become more efficient. My own view is that we can't do much about our increasing population, but we can make sure the way we produce and distribute resources is as effective and fair as possible.

Page 1 of 1   192 words   110%

3 WRITING

a Write an essay for and against the topic "Richer countries should give aid to developing countries." Use the following structure:

- Introduction – state the problem
- Arguments for giving aid
- Arguments against giving aid
- Conclusion – summarize the main points and give your opinion

1 READING

a Read the article about optimistic people. Check (✓) the correct summary of the author's ideas.

1 ☐ It's usually impossible to be an optimist if you are not naturally positive.

2 ☐ Anyone can be optimistic if they choose to do the right things.

3 ☐ Highly optimistic people are more fun to be with.

b Read the article again. Match topics a–e with paragraphs 1–5.

a ☐ Choosing the right things to think about

b ☐ Having ambitions can help

c ☐ Keeping a record

d ☐ Rethinking your attitude to work

e ☐ Where you are, who you're with

c Read the article again. Are the sentences true or false?

1 Optimists are both healthier and more successful at work.

2 Optimists focus on the happiness that the money they earn can bring.

3 It's easier to think about bad things that have happened to you than good things.

4 The writer suggests that if you believe in something enough, you'll definitely achieve what you want.

5 The writer says that writing a diary can help you understand your negative thoughts better.

6 The article says that optimistic people are lucky because they are naturally very positive.

d Write a paragraph about staying positive. Remember to include:

- what makes you feel positive
- what makes you feel less positive
- what you do if you want to improve your mood.

The **Five** **Secrets** of **Highly** **Optimistic People**

Everyone wants to be an optimist, but it's not always easy – most of us have to try hard to stay positive when life is getting us down. It's worth the effort, though, since optimists enjoy better health and even do better in their careers. Here are five things that optimists do that will help you look on the bright side, even when you're stuck in a traffic jam or forced to work on a Sunday.

The secret to optimism is that it doesn't just happen – highly optimistic people work hard to stay positive. If you want to do well in your career, improve your relationships, and enjoy your life, it's time to give optimism a try.

1 Optimists are passionate about their work. Do you need to force yourself to go to work each morning? Optimists don't because they jump out of bed excited to face the day. This is because optimists have chosen jobs and careers that they genuinely feel passionate about. If you can't remember the last time you enjoyed a day at work, it may be time to start looking for a new job. For optimists, work is more than just an opportunity to earn money. It's also an opportunity to learn, grow, and do what they love.

2 Optimists focus on good things, even though it's not the easiest thing to do. According to Florida State University professor Roy F. Baumeister's article, "Bad Is Stronger Than Good," it's much easier to focus on the rainy days than the sunny ones. In the paper, Baumeister says people are generally more upset about losing $50 than they are happy to gain $50. When you start to feel bad-tempered or depressed, think about something good from your day to balance out the negative emotions. Optimists make a choice to focus on the good in their life instead of thinking about the bad.

3 Optimists are more likely to be adventurous and ambitious. Believe in your dreams – and if you have big dreams, you might achieve better results. In 1997, researcher Gary McPherson studied child musicians, their goals, and what happened to them later in life. He found that the child musicians who imagined themselves playing their instrument forever were more likely to become professional musicians in the future. So, while belief on its own isn't enough for success, a little dreaming certainly won't hurt.

4 Optimists keep a diary. As we've mentioned, it's very easy to focus on the negative events in our lives and ignore the positives. Keeping a diary can help you release negative energy and focus on positive emotions. During a few quiet moments in your morning or before bed, write a list of the positive moments from your day or things you're trying to achieve for the future.

5 Optimists surround themselves with good feelings. If you surround yourself with supportive people and things you enjoy, you'll improve your mood and your day. The next time you lose concentration and start looking at videos of cats and dogs on the Internet, don't feel so bad about the time you wasted. Research has shown that spending a few moments doing something you enjoy will actually make you more productive.

2 LISTENING

a ▶️05.07 Listen to a conversation between two friends, Andrew and Carla. Check (✓) the things they talk about.

1 ☐ a new supermarket   4 ☐ food choices
2 ☐ packaging   5 ☐ technology
3 ☐ air travel   6 ☐ animal conservation

b Listen again and check (✓) the correct answers.

1 What is unusual about the supermarket Carla mentions?
   a ☐ It has very low prices compared to other supermarkets.
   b ☐ It sells different kinds of things from most other supermarkets.
   c ✓ The way it sells things is different from other supermarkets.

2 Why wouldn't Andrew want to use a supermarket like this?
   a ☐ He thinks it would be too time-consuming to shop there.
   b ☐ He doesn't want to have to use his car to get there.
   c ☐ He thinks it's safer if products in the supermarket use packaging.

3 What problem does Carla <u>not</u> mention related to the use of packaging?
   a ☐ the pollution it causes when it is manufactured
   b ☐ the risk it causes to animals if they eat it
   c ☐ the fact that it is often not dealt with properly after it has been used

4 What does Carla say about the idea of never using a car?
   a ☐ It's probably impossible.
   b ☐ It's difficult, but not impossible.
   c ☐ Most people wouldn't agree to do it.

5 Which of the following statements is true about Andrew?
   a ☐ He didn't know about the positive environmental impact of vegetarianism.
   b ☐ He doesn't agree with people not eating meat.
   c ☐ He is going to try to reduce the amount of meat he eats.

6 Which of the following statements best summarizes Carla's views on the environment?
   a ☐ We need to discuss what we can do to help the environment more often.
   b ☐ People in general aren't doing enough to help the environment.
   c ☐ People will probably start changing their behavior when they realize how serious the situation is.

7 How hopeful is Carla about the chances of new technology solving environmental problems?
   a ☐ very hopeful
   b ☐ generally hopeful
   c ☐ not very hopeful

c Write an email to a newspaper about a global problem that you are worried about. For example, you could talk about how pollution is a major problem all over the world. Remember to include:
• a short description of the problem
• why the problem worries you
• a possible solution to the problem
• why the problem might be difficult to solve.

👁 Review and extension

1 GRAMMAR

Check (✓) the correct sentences. Correct the wrong sentences.

1 ☐ Please write as soon as possible to me.
     Please write to me as soon as possible.
2 ☐ Probably she has been waiting for this news all week.
3 ☐ Your trip to Antarctica won't certainly disappoint you.
4 ☐ It's not likely that she will persuade her parents.
5 ☐ What will we doing this time tomorrow?
6 ☐ We hope that the problem will have been solved.

2 VOCABULARY

Check (✓) the correct sentences. Correct the wrong sentences.

1 ☐ We need someone responsable for this job.
     We need someone responsible for this job.
2 ☐ I always thought Tom was relyable until this latest incident.
3 ☐ I prefer to talk to Ann because she is more sympathetic.
4 ☐ If your desk is always neat, you're probably organized well.
5 ☐ Pollution has led to the climate change in many areas.
6 ☐ Most things we do leave some kind of carbon footprint.

3 WORDPOWER *side*

Complete the sentences with the expressions in the box.

both sides   from side to side   nice side
~~side by side~~   to one side

1 Developed countries need to work _side by side_ to help the developing parts of the world.
2 Emma seems a little cold sometimes, but she definitely has her _____.
3 In this essay, you need to present _____ of the argument.
4 I was so scared – the boat was rocking _____ in the high winds.
5 The teacher took the child _____ and told her not to do it again.

🔄 REVIEW YOUR PROGRESS

Look again at Review Your Progress on p. 66 of the Student's Book. How well can you do these things now?
3 = very well   2 = well   1 = not so well

I CAN ...	
discuss possible future events	☐
prepare for a job interview	☐
discuss advantages and disadvantages	☐
write an argument for and against an idea.	☐

6A | I'M NOT GOING TO TRY TO SEE EVERYTHING

1 GRAMMAR Gerunds and infinitives

a Underline the correct words to complete the conversation.

ELENA Hi, Max, good ¹*to see / seeing* you. How's your summer?

MAX Boring! I'm looking forward to ²*go / going* back to college. ³*To sit / Sitting* in front of the computer all day is not my idea of a vacation.

ELENA Why don't you go somewhere ⁴*to take / taking* a break? I think it's really important ⁵*to get / getting* away from everything once in a while.

MAX ⁶*To travel / Traveling* is a waste of time. I remember ⁷*to visit / visiting* Paris last spring. I tried ⁸*to see / seeing* the *Mona Lisa* in the Louvre, but there were so many people, I couldn't even get in the room, which was just as well since I'd forgotten ⁹*to take / taking* my camera. Anyway, I'm not interested in ¹⁰*walking / to walk* around in crowds of tourists.

ELENA Sorry ¹¹*hearing / to hear* that – but look, stop ¹²*to be / being* so negative. You obviously like art – that's why you went to the Louvre – so why not do something connected with that? I can see you ¹³*doing / to do* something creative.

MAX I've tried ¹⁴*painting / to paint* and I wasn't too bad at it.

ELENA There you go. You may go on ¹⁵*being / to be* in the Louvre yourself one day!

b ▶06.01 Listen and check.

c Complete the text with infinitive or gerund forms of the verbs in the box.

admire   continue   cut   have   listen   melt
pour   protect   stop   think   ~~turn~~   visit

Welcome to Niagara Falls! This is your personal audio guidebook. Remember ¹ *to turn* the volume up high because it's pretty noisy here. You can hear the water ² _____ down the falls, millions of liters every minute. If you want ³ _____ the view, press the red button ⁴ _____ the guide, and then the blue button ⁵ _____ and go on ⁶ _____ . It's amazing ⁷ _____ that the falls have been here for 10,000 years. Basically, ice ⁸ _____ into the Niagara River made it powerful enough ⁹ _____ a huge piece out of the rock. More about this later. Back to today: millions of tourists come ¹⁰ _____ the falls every year. ¹¹ _____ so many visitors is great, but all the activity causes a lot of damage, so we are trying ¹² _____ the falls as much as possible. So …

d ▶06.02 Listen and check.

2 VOCABULARY Travel and tourism

a Read the definitions. Reorder the letters to make travel and tourism adjectives.

1	not easily forgotten	e m b o e a m r l	*memorable*
2	unusual and foreign	t o e x i c	_____
3	something you admire	i p e s v i m e r s	_____
4	extremely attractive	u n s g n t n i	_____
5	the only one of its kind	e u q i n u	_____
6	very high quality	e s b r u p	_____
7	really surprising	n a i s o s t i n h g	_____
8	very noticeable	a r m b a k e e r l	_____

b Complete the text with the words in the box. There are two extra words you do not need.

structures   features   lobby   outskirts   ~~setting~~
studio   terminal   patio   hiking   venue

The Palomar Hotel is located in a perfect ¹ *setting* on the ² _____ of Phoenix just half an hour away from downtown and minutes from the ³ _____ trails going up into the Phoenix Mountains. It's an ideal conference ⁴ _____ with a number of ⁵ _____ delegates will appreciate. Whether you're outside relaxing on the ⁶ _____ admiring the views over coffee, or inside in the ⁷ _____ bar, you'll feel completely at home. In fact, why not book a ⁸ _____ apartment so that it really is a home away from home?

c ▶06.03 Listen and check.

3 PRONUNCIATION Consonant groups

a Look at the underlined syllables and decide if they contain 2, 3, or 4 consonant sounds. Check (✔) the correct box.

		2	3	4
a	We had some su<u>perb</u> meals at an excellent local restaurant.		✔	
b	These ideas are a big con<u>trast</u> to what we heard yesterday.			
c	The Pyramids in Egypt are the most impressive <u>struc</u>tures I've ever seen.			
d	Their <u>discus</u>sion lasted two hours.			
e	We can't de<u>stroy</u> the original document.			
f	The train <u>ter</u>minal is a short walk from the airport.			

b ▶06.04 Listen and check.

6B | ABOUT HALF THE WORLD'S LANGUAGES WILL DISAPPEAR

1 GRAMMAR The passive

a Underline the correct words to complete the text.

Speak any language in 30 days! That's right, with our new online course, any language can ¹*be learned / have been learned* effortlessly. This is made possible ²*with / by* an amazing piece of software that ³*has been used / is being used* today by thousands of people studying 25 different languages in the comfort of their own homes.

It's so simple. All the work ⁴*is done / is being done* online, and the course is complete. No expensive extras have ⁵*to be bought / been bought*. But don't listen to us; listen to our customers:

"I ⁶*am promoted / was promoted* back in January, but I needed to improve my English. This course ⁷*has been recommended / had been recommended* to me by a coworker, so I bought it and the results were amazing! Now I ⁸*am considered / am being considered* for an overseas position, and I'm hoping my salary ⁹*will be increased / was increased*." (Jack Lee, 32)

"I ¹⁰*have been given / am given* a completely new direction in life by this course. Now I can communicate with people all over the world. I'm so glad I ¹¹*was persuaded / am persuaded* to sign up." (Mabel Smith, 89)

What are you waiting for? Send us an email and you ¹²*are contacted / will be contacted* by our customer care team within 24 hours.

Goodbye! ¡Adios! Poka! Ciao!

b ▶ 06.05 Listen and check.

c Complete the sentences with the correct passive form of the verbs in parentheses.

1 English __is spoken__ (speak) all around the world nowadays.
2 The ancient manuscript _____ (write) many years ago in an unknown dialect.
3 Many foreign words _____ (add) to English over the centuries.
4 And that was the last word to _____ (speak) in the language of Bo.
5 All the smaller languages _____ (lose) one day, which is very sad.
6 There are free online courses, but _____ people _____ (encourage) to take them?
7 Right now a new online dictionary of medical terms _____ (made) for doctors.
8 The language _____ (not / hear) on the island for years before its revival began.
9 The pronunciation of any language _____ (make) out of a fixed number of possible sounds.
10 There is no doubt that grammar should _____ (teach) to children in schools today.

2 VOCABULARY Describing change

a Underline the correct words to complete the sentences.

1 Membership numbers began to *decline / disappear* later in the year.

2 The dodo *deteriorated / died out* due to human interference.

3 As you can see, eventually viewing figures *decreased / increased*.

4 Happily, sales are starting to *decline / revive* after a disappointing start.

5 My relationship with my boss began to *deteriorate / preserve*.

6 The ship *died out / disappeared* at sea and was never seen again.

b Complete the conversation with the noun form of the words in parentheses.

A Professor, why is it important to keep languages alive?
B Because the ¹ __survival__ (survive) of languages means the ² _____ (preserve) of cultures, too.
A Are many languages being lost?
B You can see the ³ _____ (disappear) of smaller languages all the time.
A Can you give any examples?
B Belorussian, the language in Belarus, hasn't died out, but it is in decline and future ⁴ _____ (generate) might not speak it at all.
A What about the opposite?
B There has been a ⁵ _____ (revive) of Cornish, a Celtic language.
A But what causes language ⁶ _____ (lose)?
B Basically, ⁷ _____ (compete) with bigger languages. The increase in English as a major international language is a massive factor. The effect goes beyond just language.
A What do you mean?
B Well, globalization can also mean a ⁸ _____ (deteriorate) in local customs.
A That sounds depressingly true.

c ▶ 06.06 Listen and check.

6C EVERYDAY ENGLISH
Do you mind if I ask you a favor?

1 USEFUL LANGUAGE
Introducing requests; Showing you are grateful

a Complete the exchanges with the sentences in the box.

> Do you mind if I ask you to get my coat?
> Great! I don't know how to thank you.
> Hi, Rosie. There's an idea I'd like to run past you.
> I was wondering if you wouldn't mind helping me with something?
> ~~I hope you don't mind my asking, but are you around this weekend?~~
> I'm really sorry to ask you this, but could you give me a ride home?

1 **A** <u>I hope you don't mind my asking, but are you around this weekend?</u>
 B Yes, I am. Do you need a favor?
2 **A** _____
 B What's that?
3 **A** _____
 B No, not at all. What is it?
4 **A** _____
 B Oh, don't worry about it.
5 **A** _____
 B No problem, where is it?
6 **A** _____
 B Sure, let's go.

b ▶06.07 Listen and check.

c Complete the conversation. Write one word in each space.

MARION Good to see you, Derek! Do you mind ¹_____ if _____ I ask you something?
DEREK No, ²_____ at all. Go ³_____ ahead.
MARION I hope you don't mind my ⁴_____, but I was ⁵_____ if you wouldn't mind writing a few words for the club website? We're trying to get members' profiles on there.
DEREK Sure, that sounds good. I'm happy to ⁶_____. Just tell me what kind of thing you'd like.
MARION Super, I really ⁷_____ it.
DEREK It's no ⁸_____ at all.

d ▶06.08 Listen and check.

2 PRONUNCIATION Sound and spelling: Consonant sounds

a ▶06.09 Listen and circle the correct consonant sound for the <u>underlined</u> letters.

1 I'm not <u>s</u>ure people watch as much televi<u>s</u>ion as they used to.
 <u>s</u>ure /ð/ /s/ /ʒ/ (/ʃ/) /tʃ/
 televi<u>s</u>ion /s/ /ʒ/ /ʃ/ /tʃ/ /dʒ/

2 She's also the au<u>th</u>or of a collection of <u>ch</u>ildren's books.
 au<u>th</u>or /θ/ /ð/ /ʃ/ /tʃ/
 <u>ch</u>ildren's /s/ /ʃ/ /ʒ/ /tʃ/ /dʒ/

3 The damage to our fra<u>g</u>ile environment has several cau<u>s</u>es.
 fra<u>g</u>ile /ʃ/ /ʒ/ /tʃ/ /dʒ/ /tʃ/
 cau<u>s</u>es /ð/ /s/ /z/ /ʒ/ /dʒ/

4 I never got to know her nie<u>c</u>e very well, <u>th</u>ough.
 nie<u>c</u>e /s/ /z/ /ʃ/ /ʒ/ /tʃ/
 <u>th</u>ough /θ/ /ð/ /ʃ/ /ʒ/ /dʒ/

5 The report sug<u>g</u>ests taking a fresh look at the heal<u>th</u>care system.
 sug<u>g</u>ests /θ/ /ʃ/ /ʒ/ /tʃ/ /dʒ/
 heal<u>th</u>care /θ/ /ð/ /s/ /tʃ/ /dʒ/

6 It's an adven<u>t</u>ure story that starts with the main character in pri<u>s</u>on.
 adven<u>t</u>ure /θ/ /z/ /ʒ/ /tʃ/ /dʒ/
 pri<u>s</u>on /s/ /z/ /ʃ/ /ʒ/ /dʒ/

7 There was a lot of confu<u>s</u>ion and embarra<u>ss</u>ment when I asked the question.
 confu<u>s</u>ion /s/ /z/ /ʃ/ /ʒ/ /dʒ/
 embarra<u>ss</u>ment /s/ /z/ /ʃ/ /ʒ/ /dʒ/

8 I do appre<u>c</u>iate how <u>u</u>rgent this matter has become.
 appre<u>c</u>iate /ð/ /s/ /z/ /ʃ/ /ʒ/
 <u>u</u>rgent /s/ /z/ /ʒ/ /tʃ/ /dʒ/

9 **A** Thanks anyway for <u>ch</u>ecking.
 B It's my plea<u>s</u>ure.
 <u>ch</u>ecking /s/ /z/ /ʒ/ /tʃ/ /dʒ/
 plea<u>s</u>ure /s/ /z/ /ʃ/ /ʒ/ /dʒ/

10 Occa<u>s</u>ionally, I have de<u>ss</u>ert after dinner as a treat.
 Occa<u>s</u>ionally /s/ /z/ /ʃ/ /ʒ/ /dʒ/
 de<u>ss</u>ert /s/ /z/ /ʃ/ /ʒ/ /dʒ/

6D | SKILLS FOR WRITING
The scenery was fantastic

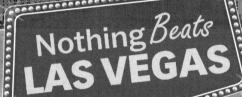

1 READING

a Read the travel blog. Are the sentences true or false?

1 The bus was cheaper than other kinds of transportation.
2 The trip to Vegas was not particularly interesting.
3 It takes a while for Vegas to make an impression on you.
4 The hotel wasn't one of the best in Vegas.
5 The magic show made a big impression on the writer.
6 Vegas is the last stage of their trip.

b Read the blog again and find five adjectives that mean *very good* or *very surprising*.

1 <u>amazing</u> 3 _____ 5 _____
2 _____ 4 _____

2 WRITING SKILLS
Using descriptive language

a Put the words in the correct order to make sentences.

1 through / absolutely / the hike on / quiet trails / the dark forest was / unforgettable .
<u>The hike on quiet trails through the dark forest was absolutely unforgettable.</u>

2 unbelievable, with / the scenery was / deep snow / absolutely / high mountains in .
_____

3 absolutely / you'll find it / easy to / get to / cheap and / mind-blowing, and it's .
_____

4 original / wooden houses / old town is / fabulous, / the / absolutely / especially the .
_____

5 this world / absolutely / recognizable because it's / the Taj Mahal / is instantly / out of .
_____

6 in their / we spent / cozy cottage / awesome day with some / an absolutely / friendly villagers .
_____

I wrote "the madness of Vegas" in my last entry, but that wasn't strong enough to describe what we found in this crazy city. We came from Lake Mead by bus, the cheapest way of getting there. That was an experience in itself because there were some amazing characters on board.

When you first come to Vegas, the sight of all those lights, massive hotels, and shopping malls is absolutely awe-inspiring. We were staying in an ordinary hotel by Vegas standards, but it was huge. I even got lost in the lobby!

There's so much to do in Vegas: the entertainment is absolutely fabulous. We went to an aquarium, a *Star Trek* museum, and a magic show, which was just mind-blowing – I think I'm starting to believe in magic now after seeing all those unbelievable tricks they do.

That was Vegas and it was really the experience of a lifetime. Our next stop is going to be somewhere a lot quieter – that won't be difficult after Vegas.

3 WRITING

a Write a travel blog about a place you've been to (different from the one you wrote about in Exercise 4 on p. 77 of the Student's Book). Use the notes to help you.

- Where you went (what kind of place is it? how did you get there? where did you stay?)
- What you did (sightseeing, entertainment, meeting people, food)
- What you saw (interesting features)
- What it was like (the good and bad points, would you recommend it?)

1 READING

a Read the article and check (✓) the correct summary.

1 ☐ Although many people think language change is bad, it is in fact normal.

2 ☐ Language change is generally negative, and we should do our best to stop it.

3 ☐ We don't know why language change happens, but it is extremely common.

b Read the article again and check (✓) the correct answers.

1 What does the writer say about language in small communities?

a ☐ Some people learn to speak better than other people.

b ✓ There is a lot of variation for many different reasons.

2 What point is the writer making when mentioning grandparents?

a ☐ That language changes over time even if people stay in the same place.

b ☐ That young people should learn the forms used by their grandparents.

3 Which of the following things do we learn when Jonathan Swift is mentioned?

a ☐ That he created a national institution to protect the English language.

b ☐ That, unlike in France and Italy, there was no national institution to protect the English language.

4 What positive aspect of language change does the writer mention?

a ☐ It allows speakers to adapt to changing situations.

b ☐ It helps make positive changes in society.

5 What does the writer suggest in the final sentence?

a ☐ Some people will always dislike how English changes.

b ☐ Language change in English will make speakers of English more creative.

c Write a paragraph about some ways your language, or a language you know well, varies. Remember to include:

• how differently young and old people speak the language
• how differently people from different places speak the language
• whether you like the differences or find any of them annoying.

Why Does Language Change?

All languages change over time, and each language varies from place to place. A language may change as a result of social or political pressures. New vocabulary is often required for the latest inventions or ideas. But a language can also change for less obvious reasons.

Influences from Other People

Language changes whenever speakers come into contact with each other. No two individuals speak the same way: people from different places clearly speak differently, but even within the same small community, people speak differently depending on their age, gender, origin, and social and educational background. When we interact with these different speakers, in different situations, we hear new words, expressions, and pronunciations, and we can make them a part of our own speech. Even if your family has lived in the same area for generations, you can probably identify a number of differences between the language you use and the way your grandparents speak or spoke. Every generation contributes to language change and when enough time has passed, the impact of these changes becomes more obvious.

Attitudes to Language Change

Jonathan Swift, the 18th-century Irish author, once wrote that we should find a way to stop our language from changing. Even today, it is common to find this idea – some people think that language should be frozen in time and protected from fashions and social trends.

Language change is often considered a negative thing. During the 18th century, Swift and many other people felt the English language was in serious decline and that a national institution – like those that existed in France and Italy – should be created to establish rules and preserve the language. Even today, we hear people complaining about a lack of "standards" in spoken and written English. New words and expressions, or pronunciations and changes in grammar, are criticized, and are often considered bad.

Change Can Be a Good Thing

Most linguists believe that change in language, like any change in society, is unavoidable. Change is a way of keeping a language alive and useful; change gives speakers different ways of saying things with extremely small differences in meaning and ways of expressing entirely new ideas. The academies established in France and Italy have had little success in decreasing the amount of change in French or Italian, and the gradual change in opinion of Dr. Johnson – a famous dictionary writer who lived at the same time as Swift – shows how ideas have developed about language change. In 1747, Johnson wrote about his desire to write a dictionary that would fix the pronunciation of English and keep it pure. But when he completed the dictionary ten years later, he admitted in his introduction that fixing a language was impossible. Like it or not, language is always changing, and English will go on doing so in many creative and – to some people – annoying ways.

Jonathan Swift

2 LISTENING

a Listen to the podcast and check (✓) the topics that the people mention.

	Mike	Samantha	Lily
sports			
music			
food			

b Listen again and check (✓) the correct answers.

1 Which reason does the presenter <u>not</u> give for why people go on staycations?
  a ☐ to save money
  b ☐ to find things near where you live
  c ✓ to have a chance to do work around the house

2 What does Mike say about what made the staycation special?
  a ☐ the visits to the exhibition and the coast
  b ☐ the small changes to how he spent his day
  c ☐ the fact he wasn't staying in a hotel

3 What do we learn about Mike and his wife?
  a ☐ They don't normally eat breakfast together.
  b ☐ They always like to have a cooked breakfast.
  c ☐ They don't have a TV.

4 Which of the following statements is true about Samantha's staycation?
  a ☐ She didn't do everything she had originally planned to do.
  b ☐ She did more exercise than she planned.
  c ☐ She repeated some of the activities on different days.

5 What does Samantha say about the food she ate?
  a ☐ She never ate takeout.
  b ☐ She ate takeout several times.
  c ☐ She only ate takeout once.

6 What do we learn about Lily's children during their staycation?
  a ☐ They didn't think the staycation was different from normal vacations.
  b ☐ They were unable to follow a rule Lily had made.
  c ☐ They played sports every day.

7 Which of the guests would recommend a staycation to the listeners?
  a ☐ Mike and Samantha
  b ☐ Mike and Lily
  c ☐ all three guests

c Write a blog post giving advice on taking a staycation in your country or hometown. Remember to include:
- a short definition of a staycation
- some suggestions of places to visit
- some suggestions of activities to do
- ideas for people who don't have a lot of money.

◉ Review and extension

1 GRAMMAR

Check (✓) the correct sentences. Correct the wrong sentences.

1 ☐ I recommend to visit Iguazu Falls as soon as you can.
    I recommend visiting Iguazu Falls as soon as you can.
2 ☐ Criminals should stop thinking about the consequences of their actions.
3 ☐ We're trying saving money for a new car.
4 ☐ Getting up at 6:00 in the morning is not my idea of fun.
5 ☐ The topic has been discussed on the show last night.
6 ☐ A new ticketing system is being introduced.

2 VOCABULARY

Check (✓) the correct sentences. Correct the wrong sentences.

1 ☐ Sally's score on the test was really impressing.
    Sally's score on the test was really impressive.
2 ☐ The movie finishes with a dramatical last scene.
3 ☐ The scenery is stunning, especially on a clear day.
4 ☐ There has been a 10% increase of profits.
5 ☐ There has been a revivation of interest in photography.
6 ☐ People hardly notice the disappearing of languages.

3 WORDPOWER *out*

Complete the sentences with the words in the box. There are two extra words you do not need.

burn	chill	fall	turn	run	~~pass~~	stand	work

1 It was such a shock that for a moment I thought I was going to ___*pass*___ out on the floor.
2 Can anybody _____ out the answer to number six?
3 We used to _____ out about really stupid things, like whose turn it was to feed the cat.
4 None of these new songs really seem to _____ out.
5 You're going to _____ out if you don't take a break soon.
6 I like to _____ out by lying on the sofa and listening to country music.

🔄 REVIEW YOUR PROGRESS

Look again at Review Your Progress on p. 78 of the Student's Book. How well can you do these things now?
3 = very well   2 = well   1 = not so well

I CAN ...	
discuss choices	☐
discuss changes	☐
introduce requests and say I am grateful	☐
write a travel blog.	☐

7A THERE'S VERY LITTLE TRAFFIC

1 GRAMMAR *too / enough; so / such*

a Complete the sentences with *too much, too many, enough, not enough, so,* or *such.*

1 It's ___not___ big ___enough___!

2 This was _____ a good idea.

3 Have you been eating _____ _____ junk food?

4 Flights are _____ cheap now that I take six trips a year.

5 I don't have _____ vowels.

6 Paula made _____ _____ mistakes.

b Complete the text with *too much, too many, enough, not enough, so,* or *such.*

Sleep debt means you don't get [1] ___enough___ sleep. The causes are obvious – [2]_____ work and [3]_____ rest basically – but what are the symptoms? Well, do you ever feel [4]_____ tired in the middle of the day that you can't keep your eyes open? Do you ever get [5]_____ bad headaches that you have to lie down for a while? Does this sound like you? If so, you need to do something about it. Actually, you don't need much sleep to recover from the day, but you should make sure you get [6]_____ rest – at least seven hours each day. In fact, [7]_____ sleep, more than nine hours, can be as bad as [8]_____ sleep, six hours or less. It is a good idea to take an afternoon nap, a siesta, especially if you can't get [9]_____ hours during the night. Some people say they feel [10]_____ refreshed after a nap that they can do twice as much. By the way, don't try not to sleep at all – people have died after [11]_____ days without sleep. Take my advice and go to bed right away!

c ▶ 07.01 Listen and check.

2 VOCABULARY Describing life in cities

a Match 1–7 with a–g to make sentences and questions.

1 [g] There is good public
2 [ ] Plans for a new highway have upset local
3 [ ] I'm not sure that the quality of
4 [ ] But should urban
5 [ ] A familiar problem is traffic
6 [ ] You can experience air
7 [ ] Get there early because parking

a congestion at rush hour.
b development come at the cost of the environment?
c life has changed much with technology.
d pollution even in smaller towns.
e residents, and they plan to protest.
f spaces are few and hard to find.
g transportation, including a tram system.

b Complete the text with the expressions in the box.

air pollution   local residents   parking space
public transportation   quality of life
traffic congestion   urban development

There is a lot of criticism of big cities, and in many ways, they are soft targets. When you're driving through a major city, the [1]traffic congestion gives you a lot of time to think, as does the time spent looking for a [2]_____. You should consider the option of living in a small town. There you would really need your car because [3]_____ is almost non-existent outside major residential areas, and nearly everything, such as the kids' schools or the supermarket, would be a drive away. Let's hope you get along well with the [4]_____ because you'll be seeing a lot of the same faces in the same places. Of course, with all that fresh air, the [5]_____ must be better, but at the same time, you'll miss all the sights and sounds of the big city. It makes you think, doesn't it? So roll down your window, breathe in that [6]_____, and be grateful for [7]_____.

c ▶ 07.02 Listen and check.

7B | I COULD HAVE IT DONE BY A PROFESSIONAL

1 GRAMMAR Causative *have / get*

a Check (✓) the correct sentences to match the pictures.

1 a ✓ She sent a message.
  b ☐ She had her message sent.

2 a ☐ He tied his hands.
  b ☐ He had his hands tied.

3 a ☐ She stole a car.
  b ☐ She got her car stolen.

4 a ☐ The crocodile took a tooth out.
  b ☐ The crocodile had a tooth taken out.

5 a ☐ The nurse took some blood.
  b ☐ The nurse had some blood taken.

6 a ☐ The boy ate a hot dog.
  b ☐ The boy had his hot dog eaten.

b Rewrite the sentences using the correct forms of *have* or *get*.

1 Somebody broke into our house. (get)
  Our house got broken into.

2 A photographer is taking my picture. (have)
  _____

3 They check patients' temperature twice a day. (get)
  _____

4 A man will fix my watch. (have)
  _____

5 Chocolate covered the boy's face. (get)
  _____

6 The hairdresser was cutting my hair. (get)
  _____

7 My wife's jewelry has been stolen. (have)
  _____

8 The workers had painted our fence red. (have)
  _____

9 The branches tore her jacket. (get)
  _____

10 I'm renewing my passport. (have)
  _____

2 VOCABULARY Movies and TV

a Complete the text with the words in the box.

> broadcast captured cast editors episode
> released script ~~series~~ shots soundtrack

New Drama

Park Hospital, the best drama [1] _____series_____ on TV, returns Monday with the first [2] _____ of season five. For those of you who don't know, here's some background: Park Hospital witnessed the good and the bad of New York City in the 1970s and '80s — its brave doctors and nurses confronted some of the city's worst crime and disease. Their stories are now [3] _____ on screen with a [4] _____ written by screenwriter Ben Goldberg and a [5] _____ of household names. The stories come to life against beautiful [6] _____ of New York City and the original Park Hospital. And *Park Hospital* is now [7] _____ all over the world. In fact, the first four seasons were recently [8] _____ on many international streaming services. To make this show appropriate for all ages, some scenes were cut by our [9] _____ because they dealt with topics that not all viewers may be ready for. We want the whole family to watch! So on Monday, when you hear that familiar [10] _____ come on, make sure you join us to watch the best drama on TV.

b ▶ 07.03 Listen and check.

3 VOCABULARY Houses

a Reorder the letters to make words.

1 a barrier between two areas of land   e n e f c   _____
2 a small house, usually in the countryside   t t a c o e g   _____
3 a space in the wall for a fire   e p a f e r i l c   _____
4 an area outside a house with plants   n d e g r a   _____
5 a narrow road between two buildings   y l a l e   _____
6 a building for a car   e g r a a g   _____

4 PRONUNCIATION Sound and spelling: *o*

a ▶ 07.04 Listen to the story. How is the underlined letter *o* pronounced in each word in the box? Complete the chart.

> sec<u>o</u>nd   f<u>o</u>r   l<u>o</u>ve   t<u>oo</u>   rep<u>o</u>rts   gh<u>o</u>st   m<u>o</u>st   T<u>o</u>wer
> L<u>o</u>ndon   sh<u>ou</u>ted   s<u>o</u>   s<u>o</u>ldier   thr<u>ou</u>gh   <u>ou</u>t

Sound 1 /ɔ/ (e.g., *four*)	Sound 2 /u/ (e.g., *food*)
Sound 3 /ə/ (e.g., *professor*)	**Sound 4 /ʌ/ (e.g., *some*)**
Sound 5 /aʊ/ (e.g., *now*)	**Sound 6 /oʊ/ (e.g., *road*)**

7C EVERYDAY ENGLISH
We could have a table or something here

1 USEFUL LANGUAGE
Imagining how things could be

a Put the words in the correct order to make sentences.

1 plates / could / and / have / we / things here .
   <u>We could have plates and things here.</u>

2 for / could / kids to / the / play / a place / be / this .
   _____

3 this / great / a / nightstand / make / would .
   _____

4 can / barbecue / I / imagine / a / having / here .
   _____

5 there / shelves / books / be / some / for / could .
   _____

6 I / enough / can't / big / imagine / being / room / this .
   _____

7 have / done / we / professional / could / it / a / by .
   _____

8 other / would / in / room / have to / that lamp / go / the .
   _____

2 CONVERSATION SKILLS
Using vague language

a Put the words in parentheses in the correct place in each sentence.

1 This could be a playroom for the twins. (kind of)
   <u>This could be a kind of playroom for the twins.</u>

2 We could put our shoes in this box. (and things)
   _____

3 I can imagine this as a desk. (or something)
   _____

4 This is where all the toys, games, go. (and things like that)
   _____

5 I guess it could be a bulletin board. (sort of)
   _____

6 The small room would make a spare bedroom.
   (or something like that)
   _____

7 There's a lot of junk here: old newspapers, broken toys.
   (and so on)
   _____

8 Put a book under the table so it doesn't fall over.
   (or something)
   _____

3 PRONUNCIATION
Stress in compound nouns

a ▶ 07.05 Listen to the sentences. <u>Underline</u> the stressed words in the compound nouns in **bold**.

1 Local residents are getting worried about the **crime rate**.
2 There's a new **shopping mall** just outside of town.
3 She said the **living room** was cozy, but really, it was just small.
4 Everyone should know the threat of **climate change** by now.
5 The **police officers** are working closely with the local community.
6 We put a **solar panel** on the roof to cut energy costs.
7 Disneyland is probably the best-known **amusement park**.
8 You can never find a **parking space** when you need one.
9 Pour it down the **kitchen sink** if you don't want it.
10 More could be done to help **developing nations** and build a better educational system.

7D SKILLS FOR WRITING
There is a great deal of concern

1 READING

a Complete Amelia's email of complaint with the words in the box.

> concern   least   prompt   reaction
> ~~regarding~~   request   residents   step

b Read the email again. Are the sentences true or false?

1 Amelia found out about this through local residents.
2 The news doesn't come as a big surprise.
3 The library has been getting less popular.
4 A journalist helped Amelia make a complaint.
5 An answer in eight days would not satisfy Amelia.
6 The council's decision is possibly illegal.

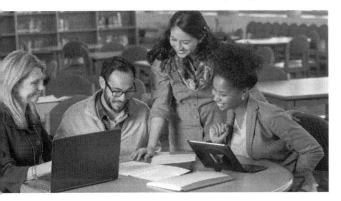

To: Ringway Council

Subject: Closure of Ringway Library

To Whom It May Concern,

I am writing ¹ _regarding_ the council's decision to close Ringway Library, as announced in the *Ringway Guardian* on Monday.

Among those of us who use the library on a regular basis, there is a great deal of ² _____ about the impact this will have on local ³ _____ who need library services. The decision comes as a shock to us, particularly as statistics show that the number of people using the library rose by 20% this year.

My first ⁴ _____ was to contact the journalist at the *Ringway Guardian* who wrote the piece, and he gave me your contact details. I have tried to call, and I even visited your offices in person, but no one was available to meet me.

I believe that it is unreasonable and unfair to close the only library in the area. My ⁵ _____ is that at the very ⁶ _____ you hold a meeting to debate the issue.

If I do not hear from you within a week, my next ⁷ _____ will be to get legal advice. I am not convinced that this decision is in line with local government guidelines.

I look forward to a ⁸ _____ reply.

Best regards,

Amelia Shaw

---

2 WRITING SKILLS
Using formal language

a Are the expressions formal or informal? Check (✓) the correct box.

		Formal	Informal
1	Thank you for your prompt response.	✓	
2	I think …		
3	I believe …		
4	The thing that really makes me angry …		
5	How about sending me a replacement?		
6	I would appreciate a replacement.		
7	Great to hear from you.		
8	Sincerely,		
9	What worries us most of all …		
10	Get back to me in a few days or …		
11	I am writing regarding …		
12	Regards,		
13	If you do not respond within three days …		
14	This is about …		

3 WRITING

a You have just found out that your local government plans to turn a children's playground near your house into a parking lot because of a lack of parking spaces. Write a formal email to complain. Use the paragraph structure and the notes to help you.

> Paragraph 1: explain your reason for writing and give details (e.g., how you found out about this)
>
> Paragraph 2: indicate why you are concerned or annoyed (e.g., children have few safe places to play)
>
> Paragraph 3: describe what action you have taken (e.g., had a meeting with neighbors who have children)
>
> Paragraph 4: explain what action you want the local government to take
>
> Paragraph 5: say what action you will take if there's no response

1 READING

a Read the article about DIY (Do It Yourself) – the activity of building, decorating, or doing repairs yourself in your own home. Match people 1–4 with activities a–d.

1 ☐ Matt   2 ☐ Esteban   3 ☐ Sarah   4 ☐ Marina

a doing someone a favor
b doing something they thought would be easy
c fixing a problem that had existed for a long time
d trying to make something more organized

b Read the article again and check (✓) the correct answers.

1 What do we learn from the first paragraph about the people who responded to the survey?
   a ☐ Five of them had damaged their home while doing DIY.
   b ✓ Most of them had failed to complete at least one DIY task.
   c ☐ Half of them plan to do one DIY job in the near future.

2 Why does Matt think he was lucky?
   a ☐ because he could have caused more damage to his house than he actually did
   b ☐ because he could have hurt himself more seriously than he actually did
   c ☐ because he was still able to finish his DIY work

3 What do we learn about Esteban's friend?
   a ☐ She had to pay for two separate things as a result of Esteban's accident.
   b ☐ She was partly to blame for Esteban's accident.
   c ☐ She was very angry with Esteban because she felt he had been stupid.

4 What was the original cause of Sarah's accident?
   a ☐ having to move a pile of books that was far away
   b ☐ resting her foot in an inappropriate place
   c ☐ hitting part of her body against something

5 Which of the following is **not** true about Sarah?
   a ☐ She eventually finished the DIY task.
   b ☐ She had to pay for the damage to be repaired.
   c ☐ She had a lot of cleaning work to do after the accident.

6 What does Marina suggest about the mistake that caused the accident?
   a ☐ It was caused by her laziness.
   b ☐ She probably wouldn't have made the same mistake during the daytime.
   c ☐ She was lucky the mistake didn't lead to a more serious problem than it did.

c Write a paragraph about a time you or somebody you know had a problem while trying to fix something. Remember to include:
   • the task you or the person was trying to do
   • whether you or the person expected it to be difficult or easy, and why
   • the problem that occurred, and the consequences of it.

DIY Troubles

Spring is nearly here and many people will turn their attention to DIY. But a recent survey has found that over 50% of people in the U.K. admit that they have at least one unfinished job to do in their home, while one in five people say they have caused damage to their home while trying to "do it themselves." Here's a selection of our readers' own DIY nightmares.

Matt I was doing a pretty simple task – just putting up some shelves in the basement of my house. I was standing on a wooden table, putting a screw into the wall and suddenly I heard a bang, and the screwdriver just flew out of my hands. Then, I noticed that all the lights had gone out. I realized there was an electric cable in the wall where I was putting the screw in. I think I was lucky – I could have been badly hurt. But it wasn't all good luck – I had to have some repairs done by an electrician and it wasn't cheap.

Esteban Once, a friend of mine asked if I could help her paint some rooms in her house. I was painting one wall, standing at the top of a ladder. For some reason, at one point, I forgot I was on a ladder and I stepped to the side. Where I put my foot there was just air, and of course I lost my balance and fell off the ladder. Unfortunately, as I did this, I knocked the ladder over and spilled the paint all over the carpet. My friend was more worried about me than annoyed about my stupidity, but in the end she had to buy new carpet ... and she called in professionals to do the painting!

Sarah I live in an old cottage. There's a big attic and it was a real mess – full of piles of old books, bags of clothes, everything. So I decided I would clear it all out and put in some cupboards and drawers to keep everything in order. I didn't get very far – after just a few minutes, I banged my head on the roof while I was trying to move a pile of old books. This made me jump back, and I put my right foot through the ceiling below. To try and get my balance, I stepped forward and my whole left leg went through the ceiling. It took days to clean up the mess in the rooms below, and I had to get the two huge holes fixed by a professional. In the end, I decided to leave the attic messy!

Marina I had a faucet that I couldn't turn off completely – there was always a little water coming out. I kept leaving it because I was too lazy, but one night I couldn't sleep because the sound of the water was really annoying me. So I decided to try and fix it – in the middle of the night. I tried to turn off the water supply before doing anything, but it was dark, I was half asleep, and I ended up turning off the gas by mistake, instead of the water. So when I unscrewed the tap, water started spraying everywhere. I shouted so much I woke up everyone else in the house, and also the neighbors on both sides. It took a long time to clean up all the water, and we were all exhausted the next day!

2 LISTENING

a ▶ 07.06 Listen to a conversation between two friends, Sam and Julie. <u>Underline</u> the correct words to complete the sentences.

1 Sam lives *downtown / outside downtown*.
2 Julie lives *downtown / outside downtown*.
3 Sam and Julie are *completely / generally / not at all* satisfied with where they live.

b Listen again. Are the sentences true or false?

1 Julie wanted to use public transportation to meet Sam, but it wasn't practical.
2 Sam is able to travel downtown from his home without difficulty.
3 Julie and Sam do not agree about how good the entertainment opportunities downtown are.
4 Sam and Julie do not agree about the level of pollution where Julie lives.
5 Sam doesn't go to the parks downtown because they're too far from his apartment.
6 Julie is considering moving back downtown again.
7 Julie and Sam agree that for people living downtown, life is faster than for people who travel in every day.
8 Julie and Sam agree that they are both lucky to live where they live.

c Write a conversation between two people discussing the quality of life in your town. Use these questions to help you:

• How much traffic congestion is there?
• Is the public transportation good? What about the parking?
• Is there much air pollution? Are there many green spaces?
• What are the entertainment opportunities?

◉ Review and extension

1 GRAMMAR

Check (✓) the correct sentences. Correct the wrong sentences.

1 ☐ It was such small apartment that we had to move out.
   It was such a small apartment that we had to move out.
2 ☐ Don't expect too much from them.
3 ☐ I think it's already enough expensive.
4 ☐ Too many people got involved in the school play.
5 ☐ I recommend visiting the museum if there's time enough.
6 ☐ We were surprised that the kids so much enjoyed it.
7 ☐ It's a such dangerous trip just to get there.
8 ☐ I introduced myself and we had a picture took together.

2 VOCABULARY

Check (✓) the correct sentences. Correct the wrong sentences.

1 ☐ There are not enough parkings for the office staff.
   There are not enough parking spaces for the office staff.
2 ☐ The standard of life is lower because of all the pollution.
3 ☐ People will always prefer cars to publique transportation.
4 ☐ No one bothered to ask local residents how they feel.
5 ☐ The scene was cutted from the final movie.
6 ☐ The next chapter in the series will be shown on Tuesday.

3 WORDPOWER *down*

Complete the sentences with a verb.

1 I was so angry, it took me a few minutes to ___calm___ down.
2 It's time for John to find someone nice and _____ down to start a family.
3 People will think you are arrogant if you _____ down on everyone like that.
4 You should _____ down on sweets if you want to lose weight.
5 She was offered a scholarship, but decided to _____ it down.
6 All this constant complaining is starting to _____ me down.

⟳ REVIEW YOUR PROGRESS

Look again at Review Your Progress on p. 90 of the Student's Book. How well can you do these things now?
3 = very well   2 = well   1 = not so well

I CAN ...	
discuss living in cities	☐
discuss changes to a home	☐
imagine how things could be	☐
write an email to complain.	☐

8A | I'D LIKE TO START SAVING FOR A HOME

1 GRAMMAR Future real and present / future unreal conditionals

a Match 1–10 with a–j to make conditional sentences.

1 [f] If I stop eating out,
2 [ ] If I didn't need to work,
3 [ ] If I see Jim,
4 [ ] If the bank didn't charge such high interest,
5 [ ] If the price is too high,
6 [ ] If Sarah paid back her student loan any time soon,
7 [ ] If I feel generous,
8 [ ] If I were you,
9 [ ] If I worked for myself,
10 [ ] If we spend more on advertising,

a   I could have more responsibility.
b   I'd become a full-time writer.
c   I'd think about what I was doing.
d   I'd take out a bigger loan.
e   I'll return the $20 I owe him.
f   I'll save a lot of money.
g   I might give some money to charity.
h   I won't buy the apartment.
i   I'd be surprised.
j   profits can increase.

b ▶08.01 Listen and check.

c Complete the sentences with the correct form of the verbs in parentheses. Use contractions where possible.

1   If the weather ___is___ (be) nice again tomorrow,
    I ___'ll go___ (go) for a walk.
2   If money _____ (grow) on trees, inflation
    _____ (be) very high.
3   I _____ (make) the coffee if you _____
    (cook) the eggs.
4   I _____ (go) to Ancient Greece if I _____
    (can travel) back in time.
5   If I _____ (be) you, I _____ (tell) the
    truth.
6   If I _____ (can't find) my blue tie, I _____
    (wear) the red one instead.
7   So _____ (take) a taxi if you _____ (be)
    in a hurry.
8   If today _____ (be) Saturday, I _____
    (stay) in bed for a couple more hours.
9   I _____ (become) a doctor if I _____
    (have) a chance to start all over again.
10   Don't worry. If I _____ (feel) bad, I _____
    (give) you a call.

2 VOCABULARY Money and finance

a Complete the sentences with the missing words. The first letters are given for you.

1   It's a good idea to put aside some s_____ for the future.
2   We will c_____ your account the annual cost of the credit card.
3   We planned $1,500 for renovation in our b_____, but in the end it cost much more than that.
4   She's very wealthy, but she donates a lot to c_____ and other good causes.
5   Government borrowing has led to the massive national d_____.
6   The research council agreed to a _____ a grant for the project.
7   Buying your own house is a good i_____ while property prices are low.
8   After Hurricane Harry, generous d_____ are coming in from all over the world.
9   George's annual i_____ is now $70,000 with his new pay raise – but that's before taxes.

b Complete the text with the words in the box.

aside	budget	charge	debt	donations	finance
grant	income	investment	~~living~~	pay	rate

John Roberts made a ¹___living___ as a fisherman working for a big fishing company. However, John always wanted to have his own boat and business, so he put ²_____ savings for years, and when the interest ³_____ was low, he went to a bank. The bank checked the ⁴_____ that John had prepared showing sales vs. costs and then agreed to ⁵_____ the project. This meant John now had a very large ⁶_____, but he considered the boat a sound ⁷_____. Unfortunately, business became more difficult because of overfishing and environmental damage. John's ⁸_____ dropped lower and lower, and he was struggling just to ⁹_____ off the interest on his loan. Before long, the bank was starting to ¹⁰_____ him penalties for missed payments. John was desperate, and he wrote about his situation on a website for start-up companies. This worked. The local council immediately awarded John a ¹¹_____ and ¹²_____ came in from people in the area. Thanks to this, John's business survived.

c ▶08.02 Listen and check.

8B | I WOULD HAVE TOLD THE MANAGER

1 GRAMMAR Past unreal conditional; *should have* + past participle

a Put the words in the correct order to make sentences.

1 had / would / if that / have / called the police / happened / to me, I .
   <u>If that had happened to me, I would have called the police.</u>

2 had / realized if / her purse / someone / she would / have / taken .
   _____

3 been all right / if / have / gotten there / quicker, everything / might / I could / have .
   _____

4 if / find / the safe / they'd been / would / have / smarter, they / tried to .
   _____

5 Jack / hadn't / them / wouldn't / know / I / her if / introduced .
   _____

6 changed / if / a long time ago / I / you, I / have / the locks / were / would .
   _____

7 she / her neighbor / hadn't / have / been / for hours if / could / come over / lying there .
   _____

8 you / in / shouldn't / bag / have / your valuables / one / put all .
   _____

9 to prison / the judge / for / a lot longer / should / him / have / sent .
   _____

10 you / what / was / watching / should / been / have / happening .
   _____

b <u>Underline</u> the correct words to complete the sentences and questions.

1 Things would have been even worse if I *haven't* / <u>*hadn't listened*</u> to you.
2 If she had contacted me, I *would have* / *would have been* helped her.
3 What *would* / *should* you have done if they hadn't arrived?
4 I would have become the manager if I *have been* / *had been* working there as long as you.
5 If the train hadn't been late, I *can get* / *might have gotten* there on time.
6 *Would you pay* / *Had you paid* $100 if you could see the questions before the exam?
7 If you hadn't dropped your laptop, it would still *work* / *have worked*.
8 You *would* / *should* have helped if you wanted us to clean up the kitchen quickly.
9 I'm sorry. I *shouldn't* / *wouldn't* have been so rude.
10 I don't understand why Carolina said that. *Would* / *Should* you have reacted in the same way?

2 VOCABULARY Crime

a Look at the pictures. Complete the sentences with the words in the box. There are two extra words you do not need.

> bribery ~~burglar~~ judge jury
> kidnapper robber shoplifting suspect

1 The _burglar_ didn't realize there was a cat at home.

2 The police caught the _____ still in the bank.

3 It was Lisa's first experience _____.

4 The _____ brought back the baby when it started crying.

5 The _____ didn't find the court case very interesting.

6 Does this count as a present or is this _____?

b <u>Underline</u> the correct words to complete the text.

One night, I came home very late and couldn't find my keys, so I had to break [1]*into* / *through* my own house! I was climbing through a window when a woman on the street shouted, "Police! There's a [2]*burglary* / *murder*!" I got down and explained that it was my house and I wasn't a [3]*cheat* / *burglar*, but she called me a [4]*liar* / *judge*. She said that she was a [5]*robber* / *witness* and that she would give [6]*evidence* / *verdict* when I was accused [7]*in* / *of* breaking and entering. She would happily come to the [8]*trial* / *case* in [9]*prison* / *court* to testify against me. She was really excited now and went on to say that the [10]*judge* / *jury* would find me [11]*guilty* / *innocent*, and the [12]*judge* / *jury* would give me a very long prison [13]*sentence* / *arrest*. I'd have to go to a horrible prison where the prisoners [14]*murder* / *lie* one another and [15]*steal* / *burgle* their cellmates' food just to survive. She was out of breath now and just about to start again when suddenly my house keys fell out of my back pocket. I wished her goodnight and went inside my house.

c ▶ 08.03 Listen and check.

3 PRONUNCIATION
Stressed and unstressed words

a ▶ 08.04 Listen and <u>underline</u> the stressed words in each sentence.

1 It <u>should</u> have been <u>sent</u> on <u>Tuesday</u>.
2 If I had seen her, I would have shouted.
3 If you had told me, it could have been different.
4 We'd never have known if she had stayed home.
5 They shouldn't have thrown it away.
6 She shouldn't have taken my purse.

8C EVERYDAY ENGLISH
You'll find something

1 USEFUL LANGUAGE
Being encouraging

a Check (✓) the most encouraging response.

1 We'll never be able to afford it.
   a ☐ You're probably right.
   b ✓ Don't give up hope.
   c ☐ That's a fair point.
2 I'll never see her again.
   a ☐ I'm sure you will.
   b ☐ That's very possible.
   c ☐ Not in a million years!
3 It started to go wrong right from the start.
   a ☐ That's life.
   b ☐ What did you expect?
   c ☐ It might work out fine.
4 That's another opportunity lost.
   a ☐ There'll be plenty more, don't worry.
   b ☐ I'd start worrying if I were you.
   c ☐ I agree with you there, and I'd be really worried.
5 I'm really worried about this interview.
   a ☐ I'm sure it'll be fine.
   b ☐ There's no time for that.
   c ☐ How can you be so sure?
6 There's not much chance of it working.
   a ☐ There would have been if it weren't for you.
   b ☐ You never know. We might pull it off.
   c ☐ No – thanks to you. We won't try it again.

b ▶08.05 Listen and check.

2 CONVERSATION SKILLS Showing you have things in common

a Underline the correct words to complete one side of a telephone conversation.

I'm really sorry to hear about your car. The ¹*same / similar / like* thing happened to me a couple of years ago. My car was stolen right outside my house, and believe it or not, I just had a ²*same / similar / like* experience, I had my wallet stolen from my purse when I was in line at the supermarket. ... That doesn't surprise me. It was just ³*as / like* that when I called the insurance company. They kept me waiting for ages, so I know the ⁴*experience / feeling*. It was the same ⁵*with / to / by* me. What can you do? ... True, that's just like ⁶*that / as / when* Sarah's apartment was robbed. I don't know what things are coming to.

b ▶08.06 Listen and check.

3 PRONUNCIATION Word groups

a ▶08.07 Listen to the sentences from a telephone conversation. Mark one pause (//) in the correct place in each sentence.

1 Hello, // this is John Peters.
2 It's Simon again from National Bank.
3 It's 973 4124.
4 No, but thanks anyway.
5 Do you want to pay by cash or by credit card?
6 That's fine, no worries.
7 I'm sorry, but I didn't get that.
8 All the best and speak to you soon.
9 Bye, thanks for calling.

8D SKILLS FOR WRITING
I really recommend it

If you love classic cinema, you can't do better than the original 1933 *King Kong* movie, one of the most famous adventure movies ever made. One of the things I love about it is that you can watch it again and again and still feel the same drama and excitement.

The story is an interesting variation on the *Beauty and the Beast* theme, with the beast being a huge ape that is captured on an exotic island and transported to the U.S. The "Beauty" in the movie is the woman used to trick the ape. The drama really begins when the ape escapes in the U.S. and goes to look for the woman …

What makes this a great movie, both now and then, is the story – it keeps you guessing all the way through, going from the jungle to skyscrapers. The acting is also excellent, and you even start feeling sorry for the ape!

King Kong is a hugely entertaining movie for viewers of all ages, and I highly recommend it if you want to escape for a couple of hours. It might be an old movie, but it is much more powerful than the remakes and is a real classic.

1 READING

a Read the review and check (✓) the questions that the review answers.

1. ✓ What kind of movie is it?
2. ☐ Did it win any awards?
3. ☐ Is it based on a book?
4. ☐ Where does the action happen?
5. ☐ What happens in the end?
6. ☐ Is it suitable for teenagers?
7. ☐ Have there been more recent versions of the movie?
8. ☐ Does the reviewer recommend it?

b Read the article again. Are the sentences true or false?

1. The reviewer has just seen *King Kong* for the first time.
2. The reviewer describes an early inspiration for the movie.
3. According to the review, the most exciting part of the movie takes place on the exotic island.
4. The plot of the movie is completely predictable.
5. According to the reviewer, the movie has an emotional impact on the viewer.
6. *King Kong* is ideal to watch with the whole family.

2 WRITING SKILLS Organizing a review

a Read the sentences and decide if they are suitable for a review of a movie or book. Check (✓) the correct box.

	Suitable	Not suitable
1 This is really a children's book, but I am sure that many adults would enjoy it, too.	✓	
2 It's better to stream the movie so you can watch it in the comfort of your own home.		
3 The lead actor, Joshua Samson, was born in a small Australian town but moved to Hollywood.		
4 There are a lot of cooking shows on TV, but this is easily the best.		
5 Believe it or not, the movie was so frightening that I couldn't sleep after I watched it.		
6 I bought this book on a fantastic vacation I had in Greece two summers ago.		
7 There is a lot of difficult vocabulary, and that makes it hard to read.		
8 To find out what happens at the end, you'll have to watch it yourself!		

3 WRITING

a Write a review of a movie you enjoyed (or hated). You could get information online and, even better, watch the movie again in English. Use the paragraph structure and the notes to help you.

> Paragraph 1: Introduce the movie and explain why you have chosen it
>
> Paragraph 2: Outline the plot and introduce the main characters
>
> Paragraph 3: Outline the key strengths of the movie
>
> Paragraph 4: Summarize the review and give your final opinion

1 READING

a Read the article about four apps that can be used to help you manage your money. Check (✓) the correct box.

	MoneyHealth	MoneyWorker	MoneyGarden	CheckMyMoney
Totally free				
Works offline				
Works on multiple devices				

Four Great Financial Tools

Managing your money and sticking to a budget can be difficult, but there are some fantastic personal finance tools that can make our lives much easier. Here are some of the best, perfect for keeping track of your finances.

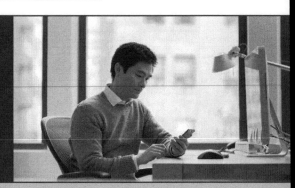

MoneyHealth

MoneyHealth instantly lets you see how healthy your finances are. It connects to your bank accounts (although at the moment, it only works with bank accounts in the U.S.) and keeps track of how much money is in each account and where your money goes. But the strength of this tool is that it does much more. It also lets you create a family budget, helps you set up goals for your savings, and even "learns" what kinds of things you're spending your money on. MoneyHealth also suggests products that might be of interest, like credit cards that could save you money. The only thing it doesn't do is actually move your money around or make payments and so on. Its function is just to describe your financial situation. Unfortunately, it's an expensive program, especially because it only works on one device.

MoneyWorker

This is an app that connects to all your devices. It keeps track of your financial transactions, such as when you use your credit card or when your bank account is charged. It also helps you create an easy-to-use budget and set financial goals. The program runs on your computer, tablet, or phone, and you have access to your financial information even if you're not connected to the Internet. But what makes MoneyWorker different is the fact that you don't just get access to software to help you manage your money – you also join a community of users around the world who can answer your finance questions and share ideas. Although this is expensive, you can try it out for free for one month.

MoneyGarden

This tool allows you to link up to almost 200 banks and other financial institutions. It produces graphs and other reports so you can see clearly when you spend your money and on what. Its application has won awards for its practical design, but like the computer program, it does need an internet connection to be useful. The program is free, but you can choose to make a donation to the creators if you find it useful.

CheckMyMoney

This is a financial tool with one main job – to create a budget for you. Once you enter the details of your bank accounts, it analyzes the data and creates a plan with a budget and suggestions for how to save money and cut your spending. Once you've set up your budget, the program helps you stick to it. The basic version of CheckMyMoney is totally free to use. However, if you want to use the added features on the app, or if you want to be able to link up more than two bank accounts, you have to pay a one-time fee to upgrade to the premium version. Users report the app can be slow when you're not connected to the Internet.

b Read the article again. Are the sentences true or false?

1 MoneyHealth can be used by people all over the world.
2 MoneyHealth isn't able to make any changes to your bank accounts.
3 MoneyWorker gives you a way of asking other people for advice about money.
4 You can use MoneyWorker for a period of time without paying.
5 MoneyGarden offers you a way to check your finances visually.
6 MoneyGarden is not suitable for people who want to check their finances while traveling.
7 CheckMyMoney can help you reduce how much you spend.
8 CheckMyMoney does not work at all unless you pay a yearly fee.

c Write a paragraph about how you manage your money. Remember to include:

- whether you are able to put aside savings regularly
- if you make a budget every week, month, or year
- if you ask anybody for advice about managing money.

2 LISTENING

a ▶08.08 Listen to a radio show about local crimes. Put the events in the order they happened.

- [ ] burglaries
- [ ] a successful arrest
- [ ] a robbery in a store
- [ ] shoplifting

b Listen to the show again and check (✓) the correct answers.

1 Which of the following statements is true about calling the show to give information?
- a [ ] You need to give your name.
- b [✓] You may earn money if the information is useful.
- c [ ] The first person you speak to when you call is a police officer.

2 What is suggested about the two men who came in the store in Monica Leonard's report?
- a [ ] They were both probably involved in the robbery.
- b [ ] The first man didn't realize what the second man was doing.
- c [ ] They left the store at the same time.

3 What do we learn about the theft at the electronics store?
- a [ ] Nobody in the store knew about it.
- b [ ] The thief attacked a young woman.
- c [ ] It happened at night.

4 What does Detective Ramirez say when talking about the burglaries?
- a [ ] The burglars took as much jewelry as they did electrical items.
- b [ ] Some of the burglaries could have been avoided.
- c [ ] The burglaries have happened in houses far apart from each other.

5 What does the presenter say about the criminals responsible for a crime previously discussed on the show?
- a [ ] No one has gone to prison.
- b [ ] Listeners helped the police identify them.
- c [ ] Some of the crimes still haven't been solved.

c Think about a crime that you have heard or read about recently. Write a short conversation between two people discussing it. Use these questions to help you:
- What was the crime?
- How did they hear about it?
- What happened?
- Did the police catch the criminal? Are they looking for them now?

◉ Review and extension

1 GRAMMAR

Check (✓) the correct sentences. Correct the wrong sentences.

1 [ ] Before you listen to my instructions, everything will be fine.
If you listen to my instructions, everything will be fine.
2 [ ] I'd be amazed if she had more children.
3 [ ] It would be a great idea that everyone biked to work.
4 [ ] Tracy would tell me if she were unhappy about it.
5 [ ] It could be nice if there were more people like her.
6 [ ] It was fantastic if you had come with us.

2 VOCABULARY

Check (✓) the correct sentences. Correct the wrong sentences.

1 [✓] It's difficult to make a living as a professional dancer.
2 [ ] One area where saving could be made is transportation.
3 [ ] The income from tourism could be much higher.
4 [ ] I'm not sure that our budjet is big enough for this.
5 [ ] There has been a large increase in donations to charities.
6 [ ] The main suspect was not the murder but someone else.
7 [ ] A man has been sentenced and will appear in court later.
8 [ ] The theif was arrested when she tried to burgle an apartment.

3 WORDPOWER *take*

Complete the text with the words in the box.

granted   pleasure   ~~charge~~   it   word   seriously

My wife goes to work and I look after our children. It made sense after her promotion, and I was happy to take
¹ ___charge___ . But take my ² _____ for it – staying home with the kids is harder than I imagined. Of course, they're my kids and I take real ³ _____ in seeing them grow up, but they need a lot of attention. When I came home from work, I took it for ⁴ _____ that they were fed, clothed, and entertained, but now I have to do all that.
I take my new role ⁵ _____, but there are days when I think I can't take ⁶ _____ anymore!

⟳ REVIEW YOUR PROGRESS

Look again at Review Your Progress on p. 102 of the Student's Book. How well can you do these things now?
3 = very well   2 = well   1 = not so well

I CAN ...	
discuss personal finance	[ ]
discuss moral dilemmas and crime	[ ]
be encouraging	[ ]
write a review.	[ ]

9A WHAT REALLY SHOCKS ME IS THAT IT COSTS $250,000

1 GRAMMAR Relative clauses

a Match 1–10 to a–j to make sentences.

1. [d] Medicine is one of those professions
2. [ ] Even today there are still diseases
3. [ ] There is research into 3D printers
4. [ ] Paramedics are basically staff
5. [ ] There may come a day
6. [ ] These pills are for patients
7. [ ] My first job was as a nurse in a private school,
8. [ ] Doctors don't have a lot of sympathy for those
9. [ ] There is medicine for an upset stomach
10. [ ] I told her to see Dr. Brown,

a that could create body parts for transplants.
b that you can buy at any drugstore.
c when machines can make blood for patients.
d where you can make a real difference.
e that there is no known cure for.
f which was an interesting experience.
g who is a specialist in eye surgery.
h who won't help themselves.
i who work alongside nurses and doctors.
j whose temperatures go higher than 39 degrees.

b Underline the correct words to complete the text. If no word is needed, choose Ø.

We like to think that we live in a world ¹*that / where / which* everyone has access to professional medical care ²*Ø / who / that* can take care of their needs. Unfortunately, for those ³*who / Ø / which* live in the developing world, ⁴*Ø / which / that* is about 85% of Earth's population, this is far from the case. Too often either the treatment from trained professionals ⁵*who / that / what* they need is impossible to get, or it costs money ⁶*that / what / who* they don't have. People ⁷*which / Ø / who* need treatment then often have to look for alternatives ⁸*that / whose / what* are relatively cheap and available.

There is a long tradition of using natural medicine, such as plants ⁹*which / where / whose* leaves and flowers can be used to take away pain. However, natural medicine is of limited use in situations ¹⁰*where / that / Ø* the patient is very sick. Even so, there are people ¹¹*who / which / Ø* suffer from serious diseases and ¹²*who / Ø / which* trust natural medicine more than modern methods. This may sound crazy to Westerners ¹³*who / Ø / which* have the luxury of professional help, but people ¹⁴*which / that / Ø* believe in this kind of treatment strongly enough might benefit just from the psychological effect, ¹⁵*which / that / Ø* could mean the difference between life and death.

c ▶ 09.01 Listen and check.

2 VOCABULARY Health

a Underline the correct words to complete the sentences.

1. The best way to *cure / heal / develop* a cold is to rest and drink plenty of liquids.
2. I can't play on Saturday because I'm still *caring for / getting over / treating* the flu.
3. My throat and chest feel really sore. I must have some kind of *bruise / cough / infection*.
4. Noah has a fever. He says he feels hot and cold, and his face is really *bruised / dizzy / pale*.
5. She *bumped / coughed / sneezed* to get his attention.
6. I still have a big *infection / strain / scar* on my knee from when I fell off the ladder.

b Complete the text with the words in the box.

> ached   bruise   ~~bumped~~   develop   dizzy
> get over   pass out   shiver   strained   treat

It all started when I was jogging in the park. I ¹ _bumped_ into something, fell down, and got a big ² _____ on my leg. It ³ _____ a little. I was worried I had ⁴ _____ my leg because I couldn't walk comfortably. I thought it was best to do something about it, so I looked up some advice online and decided to ⁵ _____ myself.

There was a lot of information, all pretty confusing, but I found a recipe for a special sports drink and drank a couple of liters of it. About an hour later, it hit me. I felt ⁶ _____, my head was spinning, and I started to ⁷ _____ – I couldn't hold a cup in my hands. I thought I was going to ⁸ _____, but I managed to crawl into bed. A week later, I'm beginning to ⁹ _____ it, and thank goodness I didn't ¹⁰ _____ any complications. I won't be using any of those websites again, though.

c ▶ 09.02 Listen and check.

3 PRONUNCIATION Sound and spelling: *ui*

a ▶ 09.03 Listen to the sentences and read the audioscript on p. 69. How are the underlined letters *ui* pronounced in each word in the box? Complete the chart.

> ~~br**ui**se~~   q**ui**et   bodyb**ui**lder   n**ui**sance
> fr**ui**t   s**ui**ts   g**ui**lty   inq**ui**re   req**ui**red

Sound 1 /ɪ/ (e.g., *hit*)	Sound 2 /u/ (e.g., *food*)	Sound 3 /aɪ/ (e.g., *time*)
	bruise	

9B THEY HAD NO IDEA IT WAS A FRAUD

1 GRAMMAR
Reported speech; Reporting verbs

a Read the newspaper headlines and underline the correct words to complete the text.

> **EXCLUSIVE! Robins did NOT walk around the world!**
>
> **HOW DID ROBINS DO THE WALK SO QUICKLY?**
>
> **Tell us the truth!**   **ROBINS: "No comment!"**
>
> **Robins: "You just want a good story!"**
>
> **Robins: "I HAVE NOTHING TO HIDE!"**   **EXCLUSIVE! ROBINS USED A PRIVATE PLANE!**
>
> **Robins: "I only flew a short way"**   **Robins: "I'll give you your money back"**
>
> **WE'VE BEEN CHEATED!**
>
> **Police won't take legal action**
>
> **POLICE TELL ROBINS TO TELL THE TRUTH**

Simon Robins was a hero when he walked around the world to raise money for charity, but journalists have now discovered [1]*that he didn't do* / *him not doing* it. Actually, Robins flew most of the way. Journalists wondered [2]*how had he* / *how he had* done the walk so quickly and asked [3]*him to explain* / *that he explained*. At first, Robins refused [4]*to talk* / *talking* about it, complaining [5]*that the press wanted* / *the press wanting* to get a good story, and he completely denied [6]*to have* / *having* anything to hide. However, journalists found out [7]*he had used* / *him using* a private plane, and finally Robins admitted [8]*to fly* / *flying* for part of the long trip. Robins insisted [9]*he had walked* / *to have walked* a lot of the way and promised [10]*to give* / *giving* money back to people who believed [11]*they had been* / *having been* cheated. The police have informed [12]*that* / *us that* they won't be taking legal action against Robins, but they have ordered [13]*that he gives* / *him to give* a full and correct account of his "walk" around the world.

b ▶ 09.04 Listen and check.

c Complete the reported speech sentences. Use contractions where possible.

1 "I'm staying home with my sister."
   Brian said <u>he was staying home with his sister</u>.
2 "It took three hours to get there."
   Jenny told me that _____.
3 "It may be a problem."
   The nurse thought that _____.
4 "Who are you going with?"
   My mom asked me _____.
5 "Why didn't you tell me?"
   Samuel wanted to know _____.
6 "I'm sorry I broke the vase."
   I apologized _____.
7 "Please be on time, everyone."
   The boss reminded _____.

2 VOCABULARY Verbs describing thought and knowledge

a Underline the correct words to complete the sentences.

1 "I don't understand why we can't see our doctor this week. He must be on vacation."
   Elena *had no idea* / *reminded* / *assumed* that her doctor was on vacation.
2 "After reading his book, I decided I didn't like his writing style."
   José *came to the conclusion* / *promised* / *suspected* that he didn't like that author.
3 "I've never heard of the Spanish Flu."
   James *assumed* / *suspected* / *had no idea* what the Spanish Flu was.
4 "We think the server is stealing money from that restaurant."
   They *asked* / *agreed* / *suspected* the server was stealing money.
5 "I'm so lucky to have met Paola."
   He *agreed* / *realized* / *told* how lucky he was to be with Paola.
6 "You're going to pay, aren't you, honey?"
   My husband *promised* / *assumed* / *reminded* I was going to pay.

b Complete the words in the sentences.

1 Wow, I never r<u>e a l i z e d</u> how difficult it would be to get everyone to agree.
2 The government has no i_ _ _ that he hasn't paid taxes in years.
3 Who do you s _ _ _ _ _ stole the information from the company's database?
4 I can only c_ _ _ to the conclusion that you are no longer interested in the job.
5 Zelda hasn't been to training for weeks, so I a_ _ _ _ _ she's left.

9C EVERYDAY ENGLISH
What's the big secret?

1 USEFUL LANGUAGE
Expressing uncertainty

a Put the conversation in the correct order.

- [ ] **B** I really have no idea. What in the world are you talking about?
- [ ] **A** Oh, come on! Black Street, you must remember.
- [ ] **A** The Black Street Café. We worked there one summer.
- [ ] **B** Sorry, but I have no idea who you are.
- [ ] **A** It's Tim, from Black Street.
- [ ] **B** Oh, Tim! What in the world are you doing here?
- [1] **A** Hi! Do you recognize me?
- [ ] **A** I wanted to ask you the same question.
- [ ] **B** Black Street? I don't have a clue where that is.

b ▶ 09.05 Listen and check.

2 CONVERSATION SKILLS
Clarifying a misunderstanding

a Complete the conversation. Write one word in each space.

A Here's your room. Have a nice stay.
B Umm, I understood [1] ___that___ we booked a large room.
A It is large – you should see the small rooms.
B And did I [2]_____ this wrong? I thought there was an ocean view.
A There's a nice painting of the ocean on the wall.
B There isn't even a shower!
A Have I [3]_____ something? I [4]_____ you were on vacation. You'll be outside most of the time.
B But [5]_____ you say this was a luxury hotel?
A It used to be – 20 years ago!

b ▶ 09.06 Listen and check.

3 PRONUNCIATION
Linking and intrusion

a Write the correct linking sounds that are added in the underlined phrases: /j/, /r/, or /w/.

1 I met John downtown <u>the other</u> day.   /j/
2 Do you know <u>where I</u> could find a post office? _____
3 I can't afford it. It's <u>too expensive</u>.   _____
4 That's Ben calling. Could you ask him where <u>he is</u>? _____
5 Don't leave the window open when you <u>go out</u>.   _____
6 Can you <u>play a</u> song for us on the piano?   _____
7 Don't assume <u>I earn</u> a lot of money doing this. _____
8 <u>Where are</u> you going? Come back here!   _____
9 If it's <u>so important</u> to you, you can have mine. _____
10 I do think <u>she ought</u> to explain exactly what she did. _____

b ▶ 09.07 Listen and check.

9D SKILLS FOR WRITING
People argue that it is no use at all

Keeping Sports Healthy

The conventional opinion about sports is that they have a positive influence on individuals' physical condition. However, some people claim that there are negative aspects of sports that should make us examine their contributions more closely.

It is said that there are several good reasons for playing sports. First, fitness is connected to health, and playing sports helps you lose weight and stay active. Second, we usually play sports with other people, and social interaction helps people stay mentally healthy and happy.

One argument given against sports is that they put stress on the body. Aside from extreme sports, even everyday activities like running can be harmful if you do them too much. Some people also worry about the long-term effects of various drugs and sports supplements.

Furthermore, it is claimed that the competitive element of sports, the "win at all costs" mentality, can make people aggressive. The reasoning is that in this case, sports become all about winning rather than being healthy and enjoying what you do.

In conclusion, I believe that playing sports can be a healthy and fun way of spending time if you do it in moderation and with the right spirit. The benefits of a healthy lifestyle almost certainly outweigh the disadvantages.

1 READING

a Read the essay about the value of sports in keeping people healthy and in shape. Are the sentences true or false?

1 Most people think that sports are a good thing.
2 The writer gives two reasons why sports are worthwhile.
3 Running is an example of an extreme sport.
4 Drugs only have an immediate effect on the body.
5 We should try to be the best at whatever sport we do.
6 The conclusion says that it is good to play some sports.

b Read the essay again and check (✓) the correct words to complete the sentences.

1 In the first paragraph, the writer … .
  a ✓ outlines the issue
  b ☐ summarizes the issue
  c ☐ criticizes the issue

2 In the next three paragraphs, the writer presents … .
  a ☐ the results of some research
  b ☐ their own opinion
  c ☐ different arguments

3 A key argument in the second paragraph is that sports … .
  a ☐ are the most effective way of staying slim
  b ☐ build good relationships
  c ☐ are as much about mental as physical health

4 The third paragraph uses drugs as an example of … .
  a ☐ an unknown factor
  b ☐ something necessary to reduce stress levels
  c ☐ something used too much in sports

5 The main idea in the fourth paragraph is that … .
  a ☐ professional sports are a bad example for people
  b ☐ when you play sports, it is natural to want to win
  c ☐ the main purpose of sports should not be beating others

6 In the conclusion, the writer … .
  a ☐ gives their personal opinion
  b ☐ introduces the strongest argument
  c ☐ presents a unique way of looking at the issue

2 WRITING SKILLS
Presenting a series of arguments

a Complete the sentences with the words in the box.

addition	against	~~argue~~	conclude
important	spite	suggests	unlike

1 People often ___argue___ that drug companies are too greedy.
2 This _____ that most people are unaware of the problem.
3 One argument _____ private healthcare is that it excludes some people.
4 In _____, there may not be enough doctors to help everyone.
5 To _____, both sides of the argument have some validity.
6 It's _____ not to forget that this medicine is not available everywhere.
7 In _____ of advances in medicine, we have no cure for many diseases.
8 We can eat fresh fruit year round now, _____ 50 years ago.

3 WRITING

a Write an essay on the topic "Are we healthier today than we were 100 years ago?" Use the paragraph structure and the notes to help you.

- Introduction: outline the topic
- Main argument for better health: medicine and technology, better nutrition is available
- Other arguments for: more leisure time
- Arguments against: bad diets, cars, TV, and computers, life moves too fast
- Conclusion: summarize the arguments and give your opinion

Georges Méliès

1 READING

a Read the article about Georges Méliès.
Put the events in the order they happened.

- [ ] He bought a theater.
- [ ] He developed new filmmaking techniques.
- [ ] He lived abroad.
- [ ] He made his own camera.
- [ ] He received a prize from his country.
- [ ] He saw his first movie.
- [ ] He stopped making movies.

b Read the article again and check (✓) the correct answers.

1 Méliès went to study in London … .
   - a [ ] because there was a very famous art school there
   - b [✓] because of his parents' wishes
   - c [ ] because he wanted to learn more about theater magic

2 After buying the Théâtre Robert-Houdin, … .
   - a [ ] Méliès performed shows there using things he learned in London
   - b [ ] Méliès split his time between working there and continuing his studies
   - c [ ] Méliès was able to save up a lot of money from the profits

3 After seeing the Lumière brothers' movie, Méliès … .
   - a [ ] suggested they collaborate on a project together
   - b [ ] introduced them to a filmmaker in London
   - c [ ] made them an offer that they did not accept

4 Méliès started to make his own movies … .
   - a [ ] after he was given a camera from Robert Paul
   - b [ ] using a camera he made himself
   - c [ ] after learning some techniques from Robert Paul

5 Méliès's decision to start experimenting with special effects … .
   - a [ ] was the result of an accidental discovery
   - b [ ] came after he felt unable to film a street scene in the way he wanted
   - c [ ] because he felt that other movies he'd watched were unsatisfactory

6 The writer suggests Méliès stopped making movies … .
   - a [ ] because audiences stopped going to see them
   - b [ ] because he didn't find the work interesting anymore
   - c [ ] because he wanted to work in the theater again

7 When he was older, Méliès … .
   - a [ ] was totally forgotten in France
   - b [ ] returned to making movies
   - c [ ] did not have to pay for his own accommodation

c Write a paragraph about someone famous in your country who only became well known later in their life. Remember to include:

- what the person is famous for
- what they did before finding fame
- what your opinion is of this person.

The Oscar-winning movie *Hugo* by Martin Scorsese has people around the world interested in a French director born over 150 years ago. Marie-Georges-Jean Méliès was born in Paris in 1861. From an early age, he showed a particular interest in the arts. After studying at a famous art school in Paris, Méliès continued his studies in London – his parents insisted he learn English. While in London, he developed an interest in theater magic.

When he returned to Paris, he worked at his father's factory and took over as manager when his father retired. His position meant that he was able to save enough money to buy the famous Théâtre Robert-Houdin when it was put up for sale in 1888. From that point on, Méliès worked full time, performing shows at the theater, using techniques that he studied while in London, as well as working on his own tricks.

When the Lumière brothers – said to be the first ever filmmakers – showed their film to the public for the first time, Méliès was a member of the audience. What he witnessed clearly had a strong effect upon him. After the show, he asked the Lumière brothers if he could buy their projector, but they turned him down. However, Méliès had come to the conclusion that filmmaking was his future, so he went to meet Robert Paul – a British filmmaker – in London. Méliès looked at Paul's camera-projector and built his own soon afterward. Within months, Méliès was making and showing his own movies.

In the autumn of 1896, an event occurred that changed the way Méliès looked at filmmaking. While filming a simple street scene, Méliès's camera got stuck and it took him a few seconds to solve the problem. When he later watched the movie, Méliès was amazed by the effect that the incident had on what he'd filmed – objects suddenly appeared, disappeared, or were transformed into other objects. It occurred to him that he could use techniques like this to change the appearance of time and space in his movies. He used this discovery to create complex special effects.

Méliès made a wide range of movies. He is most famous for his fantasy movies, but he also made advertising movies and serious dramas. However, after a while, audiences stopped finding his work so interesting or unusual, and in 1912, he gave up making movies. In 1915, he was forced to turn his movie studio into a theater, and he started presenting live shows again. In 1923, he ran out of money and his theater was knocked down. Méliès was almost totally forgotten, but in the late 1920s, his contribution to cinema was recognized by the French, and he was given a special award – the Legion of Honor – and a rent-free apartment where he would live for the rest of his life.

Georges Méliès died in 1938 after making over 500 movies. He paid for, produced, and starred in almost every one.

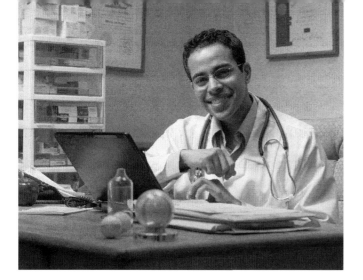

2 LISTENING

a ▶ 09.08 Listen to a conversation between a doctor and a patient. Match the three things the patient asks about 1–3 with the advice the doctor gives a–c.

1 ☐ cough
2 ☐ injuries from a bike accident
3 ☐ shots for a trip abroad

a Speak to somebody else.
b Come back if the problem doesn't go away.
c Use some medicine.

b Listen again and check (✓) the correct answers.

1 How long has the patient had his cough?
  a ☐ for two days
  b ✓ for four days
  c ☐ for a few weeks

2 What does the doctor say about the patient's cold?
  a ☐ It will probably go away on its own.
  b ☐ It will probably cause a chest infection later.
  c ☐ It may be caused by having several colds at the same time.

3 What does the doctor say about the patient's bike accident?
  a ☐ The patient probably wasn't seriously injured since he didn't pass out.
  b ☐ The patient did not do the right thing after having the accident.
  c ☐ The patient should go to the hospital now for further checks.

4 What does the doctor say the patient should do now?
  a ☐ Avoid using the bike until next week.
  b ☐ Avoid using the bike for several weeks.
  c ☐ Do the race, but very slowly.

5 What will the patient need to do if he needs shots for his vacation?
  a ☐ Return to the doctor.
  b ☐ Get the shots from someone at reception.
  c ☐ Get the shots from a nurse.

c Write a conversation between two friends who are discussing what they do when they get sick. Use these questions to help you:

- What kinds of common illnesses do they get?
- What kind of medicine do they take?
- What other things do they do to try to feel better?
- Have they ever tried a "cure" that didn't work?

⊙ Review and extension

1 GRAMMAR

Check (✓) the correct sentences. Correct the wrong sentences.

1 ☐ It was the captain of the ship which was responsible.
   It was the captain of the ship who was responsible.
2 ☐ Throw away the tables whose legs are broken.
3 ☐ The movie review, that came out yesterday, wasn't positive.
4 ☐ I moved into the room where you used to live in.
5 ☐ Then Rachel said me that she wanted to leave.
6 ☐ It's a beautiful day, so I suggest having a picnic by the river.

2 VOCABULARY

Check (✓) the correct sentences. Correct the wrong sentences.

1 ☐ Doctors are trying to develope new methods of treating patients without surgery.
   Doctors are trying to develop new methods of treating patients without surgery.
2 ☐ Marco can't race or train for three months, and he isn't treating this very well.
3 ☐ The cost of medicine is a problem in the develop world.
4 ☐ You should take care for yourself now that you're pregnant.
5 ☐ I feel weak. I'm sure I'm coming down with something.
6 ☐ Give her something before she loses consciousness!

3 WORDPOWER *come*

Complete the sentences.

1 The check at the restaurant came ___to___ over $200!
2 I came _____ an old photo of you while I was cleaning out the closet.
3 Grandma's dream has finally come _____ . We bought her the chance to drive a Formula 1 car for the day.
4 We had to throw away the entire dinner. I've come to the _____ that I am not a master chef.
5 The name Elvis has come _____ a lot today. Every visitor to the museum has asked about him.
6 We're just going to advertise our business on the Internet unless we can come up _____ a better idea.

⟳ REVIEW YOUR PROGRESS

Look again at Review Your Progress on p. 114 of the Student's Book. How well can you do these things now?
3 = very well   2 = well   1 = not so well

I CAN ...	
discuss new inventions	☐
discuss people's lives and achievements	☐
express uncertainty	☐
write an essay expressing a point of view.	☐

10A | IT MIGHT NOT HAVE BEEN HIS REAL NAME

1 GRAMMAR Past modals of deduction

a Underline the correct words to complete the sentences.

1 John's shoes are too small for the new school year. He *must / might / could* have grown a lot over the summer.
2 We *must / may / could* have moved to Australia, but we decided to stay in Canada in the end.
3 That *couldn't / may / must* have been Sheila in the car, but I'm not too sure from this distance.
4 You *couldn't / may not / must not* have eaten all the cupcakes. You'd be sick now!
5 The keys could be anywhere. I *couldn't / might / must* even have left them at the gym.
6 Wait, don't call her yet. She *might / must / might not* have woken up.
7 Poor Andrés didn't eat for 24 hours. He *could / may / must* have felt really hungry.
8 I sent him a text, but he *couldn't / may not / must not* have received it because the reception isn't very good here. I'll try again.
9 Don't be silly – there was an instructor with them. What *couldn't / could / must* have gone wrong?
10 Sophie was in bed with the flu, so she *couldn't / may not / must not* have gone to the party.

b Underline the correct words to complete the text.

Shergar was a very successful champion racehorse; in fact, he ¹*couldn't / might* have been the best ever. His racing career ended in 1981, but he ²*could / must* have made his owners a lot more money if he hadn't been stolen in 1983. Shergar was never seen again.

There are lots of theories about who took Shergar and what happened to him, but in reality, anything ³*must / may* have happened. The kidnappers ⁴*must / might* have been very professional, or very lucky, because they hid their victim so successfully. It ⁵*couldn't / must not* have been easy to steal such a famous horse and make it disappear completely. People say the police ⁶*may / must* not have done the best job looking for the horse because they ⁷*could / must* have acted a lot more quickly – but the truth is, they didn't have much evidence, and the horse and its kidnappers were never found.

Some people say the kidnappers ⁸*couldn't / must* have killed Shergar when the owners didn't agree to pay the kidnappers. This ⁹*must / could* have been a tragedy for the owners and fans of Shergar. However, there ¹⁰*must / may* have been a happier ending. Of course, Shergar couldn't be alive today because this happened so many years ago. An optimist would say that he ¹¹*couldn't / might not* have been killed by the kidnappers. He ¹²*must / could* have died a natural death somewhere safe. We will probably never know.

c ▶10.01 Listen and check.

2 VOCABULARY Adjectives with prefixes

a Complete the sentences by adding a negative prefix to the adjective in parentheses.

1 I am writing this complaint letter because I was completely _dissatisfied_ (satisfied) with the hotel facilities.
2 The product sells very well, so it's _____ (logical) to stop making it.
3 The fact that the suspect has a lot of tattoos is completely _____ (relevant).
4 Mike, this is an _____ (expected) surprise. I can't even remember the last time I saw you!
5 The view from the balcony is _____ (believable). You have to see it for yourself.
6 The laws of physics show that it is _____ (possible) to go back in time.

b Complete the text with negative forms of the adjectives in the box.

credible experienced formal honest patient
polite probable reasonable regular responsible
~~satisfied~~ successful

Sally had worked as a trainee chef at a hotel for six months, but she was already ¹_dissatisfied_ with her job, especially the ²_____ hours and ³_____ customers. Also, Sally was still pretty ⁴_____, but the head chef used to get ⁵_____ with her because she couldn't do everything. Sally started to lose her self-confidence. Did she have ⁶_____ expectations? Was she just another ⁷_____ trainee, and would it be ⁸_____ to continue at a job she couldn't do? It was highly ⁹_____ that things would get better. Sally got some ¹⁰_____ advice from an old teacher, who told her to leave. For some reason – perhaps it meant she was ¹¹_____, too – Sally didn't listen to this advice, and she stayed at the hotel. This might seem ¹²_____, but five years later, Sally is now head chef. She always smiles when her trainees tell her they want to leave.

c ▶10.02 Listen and check.

3 PRONUNCIATION Word stress

a Underline the stressed syllables in the words in **bold**.

1 The new parts are pretty **inexpensive**.
2 I find it **improbable** that they just happened to be in the same place at the same time.
3 The weather at this time of year is really **unpredictable**.
4 I won't go on a trip as **disorganized** as this one again.
5 I've dropped it on the floor a few times, but it's **unbreakable**.
6 I can do it, but it's kind of **inconvenient**, and I'm not very interested.

b ▶10.03 Listen and check.

10B | I'VE MANAGED TO MAKE A DREAM COME TRUE

1 GRAMMAR Wishes and regrets

a Underline the correct words to complete the sentences.

1 I wish I *would / could / did* speak another foreign language.
2 Do you ever wish you *had / have / would have* a brother instead of a sister?
3 I *wish / wished / hope* Sarah and Miguel get back together.
4 If only I hadn't *make / made / have made* so many mistakes in the first part of the test.
5 I wish you *would / should / might* think about somebody besides yourself.
6 I'm sure all soccer coaches wish they *were / are / would be* still able to play themselves.
7 You *would / should / will* have thought about that before you started shouting at everyone.
8 If you had three wishes, what *would / did / should* you wish for?
9 She wishes she *has / had / would have* spoken to the doctor a lot earlier.
10 Lana is nice, but I wish she *does / has done / did* more to help around the house.

b Complete the sentences. Use contractions where possible.

1 It's too bad you're not with us.
   I wish _____ you were _____ with us.
2 Jane, please listen to me for a moment.
   I wish Jane _____ for a moment.
3 I want to be ten years younger.
   She wishes that _____ ten years younger.
4 Mike doesn't live very close to downtown.
   Mike wishes _____ closer to downtown.
5 Why didn't I buy that dress?
   I wish _____ that dress.
6 It would be great if my horse wins the race.
   I _____ my horse wins the race.
7 It was wrong of me to be so rude to the sales assistant.
   I wish _____ so rude to the sales assistant.
8 It makes me so embarrassed when he lies.
   I wish _____ – it makes me so embarrassed.
9 I didn't study very hard in school, unfortunately.
   If only _____ harder in school!
10 My husband and I are watching a really boring movie.
   I wish _____ this boring movie.
11 Why didn't we go on this trip last year?
   We _____ on this trip last year.
12 It was a mistake to tell Eva.
   You _____ Eva.

2 VOCABULARY Verbs of effort

a Underline the correct words to complete the text. Then listen and check.

Fighting Shirley

Shirley Chisholm (1924–2005) was the first African American woman elected to the U.S. Congress. In 1972, she became the first African American and the first woman to [1]*work on / pursue / overcome* the Democratic presidential nomination.

Chisholm was born in Brooklyn, New York. At Brooklyn College, she excelled on the debate team, and her professors encouraged her to go into politics. She started out teaching, but she stuck [2]*on / by with / with* her passion, joining organizations that [3]*tackled / stuck with / gave up* political and civil rights issues.

In 1968, she won a seat in the U.S. Congress. There "Fighting Shirley" tirelessly worked [4]*with / by / on* civil rights issues. In 1972, she ran for president. She had to [5]*overcome / try out / pursue* plenty of racial discrimination; in fact, she was blocked from participating in the presidential debates, but she didn't give [6]*out / up / away* – she took legal action and was allowed to give one televised speech. Although she lost the nomination, she continued in Congress until 1983. She coped [7]*by / with / in* racism and sexism throughout her career, but "Fighting Shirley" will always be remembered as a woman who fought for change.

b ▶10.04 Listen and check.

c Complete the sentences and questions with the words in the box.

cope with	stick with	give up	pursue
overcome	~~tackle~~	work on	

1 I think Olivia managed to ____ tackle ____ the task very well in the end.
2 It might seem difficult now, but it's important not to _____.
3 Is Chris really going to _____ this idea of running a marathon?
4 At first I couldn't _____ the pressure of working such long hours.
5 Few people realize how many difficulties he has had to _____ to get this far.
6 I need to _____ my pronunciation if my English is going to improve.
7 Don't complain – just _____ it!

10C EVERYDAY ENGLISH
Two things to celebrate today

1 USEFUL LANGUAGE
Describing how you felt

a <u>Underline</u> the correct words to complete the sentences.

1 When they took my winning ticket out of the bag, I was so
   <u>*surprised*</u> / *disappointed* / *interested*.
2 I *shouldn't* / *couldn't* / *wouldn't* believe it. It didn't seem real.
3 Trevor was *waiting* / *expecting* / *realizing* the news, but it
   still came as a shock.
4 I was really *pleasant* / *pleasing* / *pleased*. I think I deserved
   to win first prize.
5 It was quite *a blow* / *news* / *expected*. I just stood there in
   shock.
6 The party was a disaster. I still can't *be* / *go* / *get* over it.

2 CONVERSATION SKILLS
Interrupting and announcing news

a Put the conversation in the correct order.

- [ ] **B** That's true, I guess. Well, thanks for telling me. I'd
      better get back to work.
- [ ] **B** What? I don't know about that. I'll have to think it over.
- [ ] **B** No problem, Luke. What's up?
- [ ] **B** Hold on. I just talked to Diego yesterday. He didn't say
      anything.
- [ ] **A** Well, it's true. One more thing. Diego's gone to Masons.
- [1] **A** Hi, Cleo. Thanks for coming to see me.
- [ ] **B** But. Masons is our competitor. That's a disaster!
- [ ] **A** Well, Diego has resigned.
- [ ] **A** Just a minute. There's something else we have to
      discuss. Would you be interested in taking Diego's job?
- [ ] **A** It's not a tragedy. We don't have any secrets he can tell
      them.

b ▶ 10.05 Listen and check.

3 PRONUNCIATION Consonant groups

a ▶ 10.06 Listen and <u>underline</u> the words that have
a consonant group (two or more consonant sounds
together).

> In the <u>winter</u> of eighteen fifty-five, the people of
> Devon in England woke up to find the footprints of
> a strange animal in the snow.
>
> Some frightened people followed them, and the
> footprints went on and on … for approximately a
> hundred miles – if their account is to be believed.
>
> The footprints went in a straight line through
> gardens and over walls and roofs.
>
> No one could explain the footprints, but since then
> many theories have been suggested.
>
> One of the strangest was that a kangaroo had
> escaped from a nearby zoo and jumped through the
> countryside!

1 READING

a Read the beginning of a story. Put the events in the order they happened.

- ☐ She walks to the hotel.
- ☐ Jill finds evidence the hotel isn't closed.
- ☐ She asks for help.
- ☐ Jill switches on a light.
- ☐ 1 Tony gets married.
- ☐ Jill opens a letter.
- ☐ Tony invites Jill to visit him.
- ☐ She finds where the smell is coming from.
- ☐ Jill's car breaks down.

b Read the story again and check (✓) the most appropriate answers.

1 How did Jill get to the hotel?
   a ☐ by car
   b ✓ on foot
   c ☐ It doesn't say.

2 What could Jill smell when she got there?
   a ☐ something difficult to recognize
   b ☐ something she instantly rrecognized
   c ☐ something unpleasant

3 How did Jill find the hotel?
   a ☐ by following directions
   b ☐ from memory
   c ☐ by chance

4 What happened to the car?
   a ☐ There was a technical problem.
   b ☐ There was an accident.
   c ☐ It ran out of gas.

5 Why did Jill criticize Tony?
   a ☐ He had lied to her.
   b ☐ He refused to visit her.
   c ☐ He underestimated the trip.

6 What did Jill feel guilty about?
   a ☐ having negative feelings about Tony
   b ☐ disturbing the hotel guests
   c ☐ turning on the light

7 What did Jill feel when she turned on the light?
   a ☐ relief
   b ☐ respect
   c ☐ regret

8 What stopped Jill from running out of the room?
   a ☐ She saw the message.
   b ☐ She smelled the food.
   c ☐ The door was locked.

The hotel was in darkness. Feeling tired from the walk, I stopped and looked around. What was going on? The place was obviously open – there were some cars and an unfamiliar smell from somewhere. It was strange finding a hotel – I couldn't remember seeing it on my map, but here it was.

If only my car hadn't broken down in the middle of nowhere, making me look for help. The trip hadn't been my idea. Tony had kept asking me to visit him and his new wife, and I had finally agreed. "A few hours by car, Jill," Tony had said.

I called out, "Is anybody here? I need some help with my car." Silence. Feeling guilty, I went inside. That strange smell was getting stronger, and I went toward it, almost falling down in the dark. Thankfully, I found a light switch and turned it on. I wish I hadn't.

I saw a table with a lot of food: meat, vegetables, fruit, cakes. All of it had gone bad and was rotten. Reaching for the door, I wanted to leave, but I noticed something else on that terrible table: a letter marked "For Jill from Tony." Inside, it said simply: "You were too late for the party." What could it mean?

2 WRITING SKILLS Making a story interesting

a Match 1–6 with a–f to make sentences.

1 ☐ d Walking away down the road,
2 ☐ Holding my head in my hands,
3 ☐ Shouting at the top of my voice,
4 ☐ Feeling weak and dizzy,
5 ☐ Not being in the best of moods,
6 ☐ Listening for a warning signal,

a I began to cry.
b I had to sit down for a moment.
c I hid behind a tree and waited.
d I resisted the temptation to look back.
e I sat in a corner and ignored everyone.
f I tried to get her attention.

b Complete the pairs of sentences with the gerunds and verbs in the box.

feeling / felt   ~~hearing / heard~~   hiding / hid   holding / held   realizing / realized

1 a ___Hearing___ her voice shouting "Come back," I resisted the temptation to look back at her.
   b Lying on the ground and holding my breath, I ___heard___ someone walking close to me.

2 a _____ weak and dizzy, I had to sit down for a moment.
   b It _____ good to see Ben up and walking again after the accident.

3 a Darkness came and we soon _____ that we were completely lost.
   b Not _____ my mistake, I went on as if nothing had happened.

4 a Listening for a signal, I _____ behind a tree, waiting anxiously.
   b He had a terrible day, _____ from the criminal who wanted to find him.

5 a The poor girl _____ her head in her hands, crying with frustration.
   b An old man came up, _____ a cup which he then offered to me.

3 WRITING

a Choose one of these first lines and continue the story. Write three paragraphs.

Looking into the terrible storm, I thought, "How are we going to get out of this?"

I shook his hand and hurried away, hoping I'd never see him again.

UNIT 10
Reading and listening extension

1 READING

a Read the blog about regrets. Match the people 1–5 with the regrets a–e.

1 ☐ Jon (the author of the article)
2 ☐ Amber
3 ☐ Santiago
4 ☐ Tony
5 ☐ Sofia

a an experience in college
b an experience while looking for work
c not spending time with the family
d not studying enough in school
e not traveling more

NEW POSTS | OLDER POSTS   SEARCH 🔍

ANY REGRETS? *(Posted by Jon, March 24)*

A recent survey of over a thousand men and women in the U.K. aged over 25 found that if they could go back in time, 22% of married women would choose a different husband. Only 12% of men say they should have chosen a different wife! The survey also found that 30% of people wish they had chosen a different career, 35% wish they had chosen a different major in college, and 37% wish they had saved more money. Finally, 53% said they wish they had traveled around the world more when they were younger.

I'd have to get married before I could comment on the first two statistics. But if I could go back in time, would I choose a different college major? Maybe. Would I have traveled more? Definitely, but then I think I really did all the traveling I could with the money I had. What about you? Would you have done anything different when you were younger? Do you have any big regrets?

AMBER
I do sometimes think back to one class in college. It was one of the last classes I had to take to finish my degree. I did OK in the class, but it was my last semester and I just wasn't very motivated, so I didn't pay a lot of attention and afterward, I threw away all my notes. I recently changed jobs, and my new job deals with many topics we covered in that class. I have often thought in the past few months – if only I had saved my notes and paid more attention in class! But I guess it doesn't really matter. I'm learning new things every day at work, and I don't think my life would've been that different if I had studied harder in that class and saved my notes. I suppose it would have been just a little easier for my job now.

TONY
I wish I'd spent more time with my children when they were really young. I had a high-pressure job with long hours and regular trips abroad. So, although I tried to see my children as much as possible, I devoted a lot of my time to work because I thought I should be earning as much money as possible. On weekdays, I rarely saw them because I left for work before they woke up and got back after they'd gone to bed. Unfortunately, I think it's often easier to say "no" to family than it is to work. Someone once told me: "If you lose money, you can always earn more, but if you lose time, you can never get it back." I didn't really understand what that meant at the time, but now that I'm older, I do.

SANTIAGO
Personally, I think the most important thing is to enjoy your life now and not think too much about the past and how things could have been different. I sometimes think about one job interview I went on just after finishing school. I'd planned to get the train to go to the interview, but because I prefer driving, I decided to take the car and ended up getting lost in a city I didn't know very well. So I arrived late, which didn't create a good impression, and I wasn't offered the position. I was devastated at the time, but two months later, I got a much better job. So instead of regretting, I think we should look to the future and concentrate on overcoming problems we can actually change – I think everything happens for a reason.

SOFIA
I think that when you regret something, you can use that experience to work on your weaknesses and do better in the future. You learn from what went wrong and the mistakes you made, and make sure you do things differently next time. I was really irresponsible in school. I should have studied harder. But that was a good thing, because at college, I realized my mistake, and I really worked hard and appreciated the opportunity to study there. So in that case, regret really helped me change my behavior.

b Read the blog again. Complete the sentences with the names in the box.

Jon   Amber   Sofia   Santiago   Tony

1 _____ thinks regrets are not useful.
2 _____ regrets something that was probably unavoidable.
3 _____ regrets something for professional reasons.
4 _____ says you can learn from regrets.
5 _____ understands something better now than in the past.

c Read the blog again. Are the sentences true or false?

1 More men than women wish they had chosen a different partner.
2 Jon (the writer of the article) isn't married.
3 Amber didn't do well in the class because she didn't spend much time studying for it.
4 Santiago thinks he didn't get the job because his train was late.
5 Tony generally only saw his children on the weekend.
6 Sofia thinks her lack of effort in school made her a better college student.

d Write a paragraph about a regret that you or someone you know has. Remember to include:

- what the regret is
- why you or the person chose that course of action
- how your or the person's life would be different now if something had been different then.

2 LISTENING

a ▶10.07 Listen to five people talking about recent events. Match people 1–5 with situations a–e.

1 ☐ Juan   a a car accident
2 ☐ Michelle   b a work meeting
3 ☐ Geno   c an interview for a college scholarship
4 ☐ Liam   d losing an object
5 ☐ Emily   e meeting someone on the street

b Listen to the five people again. Match the emotions in the box with the people. There are three extra words you do not need.

angry   confident   exhausted   fortunate
not hopeful   regretful   surprised   worried

1 Juan   _____   4 Liam   _____
2 Michelle   _____   5 Emily   _____
3 Geno   _____

c Write a conversation between two people discussing an event neither of them is able to explain. Use these questions to help you:

- Where and when did the story take place?
- What happened?
- Why can't they explain what happened?
- Were they with any other people? Do they have an explanation for the event?

 # Review and extension

1 GRAMMAR

Check (✓) the correct sentences. Correct the wrong sentences.

1 ☐ Thank you and I wish to hear from you soon.
     Thank you and I hope to hear from you soon.
2 ☐ We do hope you would enjoy the rest of your stay.
3 ☐ Sometimes I wish I were back in college again.
4 ☐ Goodbye, and I wish we can meet again soon.
5 ☐ Ryan wishes he spent more time there last summer.
6 ☐ Now I wish I hadn't let Chris on the team.

2 VOCABULARY

Check (✓) the correct sentences. Correct the wrong sentences.

1 ☐ My friend Jane is a very responsable person.
     My friend Jane is a very responsible person.
2 ☐ The training facilities are satisfied for a club of this size.
3 ☐ Linda is really impatient, so don't keep her waiting too long.
4 ☐ I'm very unsatisfied with your response to my recent letter.
5 ☐ The police discovered her illegally use of company funds.
6 ☐ I can't cope with all these problems. I need some help.
7 ☐ I'd like to try snowboarding while we have some snow.

3 WORDPOWER *way*

Underline the correct words to complete the exchanges.

1 **A** Do you want a ride to the station?
   B Don't worry, *there's no way / all the way / we'll make our way* after lunch.
2 **A** So Andy starts, then it's Rosie, then Amanda?
   B *One way or the other. / In some ways. / It's the other way around.*
3 **A** Would tomorrow around seven be all right?
   B *There's no way / One way or another / In some way* we can start that early.
4 **A** Is it difficult to get up the mountain?
   B No, there's a good path *the other way around / one way or another / all the way.*
5 **A** Are you sure you can get the car working again?
   B *All the way / One way or another / In some ways,* we will.

🔄 REVIEW YOUR PROGRESS

Look again at Review Your Progress on p. 126 of the Student's Book. How well can you do these things now?
3 = very well   2 = well   1 = not so well

I CAN ...	
speculate about the past	☐
discuss life achievements	☐
describe how I felt	☐
write a narrative.	☐

UNIT 1

▶ 01.01

The other day, I was walking down the street when I saw Sam Carter, you know, the famous movie director. I was really excited because he has been one of my favorite directors for years, and I watch his movies all the time. "What is he doing here?" I thought to myself. There was only one way to find out. Sam was going into a café, but I stopped him before he went inside and said, "Hi, Sam!" He smiled at me, and we started to talk outside. I couldn't believe I was talking to Sam Carter! He always looks so serious in photos, but he's a really friendly guy. In the end, Sam invited me for coffee. Then he told me why he was in town. His company was making a new movie with a lot of new faces in it, just ordinary people, but they needed some more.

"How about you?" Sam asked. "Have you watched any of my movies? Do you want to be in one?" I was so shocked, I dropped my cup and the hot coffee went all over Sam; he yelled and ran outside. I made a terrible first impression!

▶ 01.02

/ɪ/: desire, prizes, women
/e/: desert, helpful, identity, sensitive, slept
/ɜ/: concerned, dessert, prefer, service

▶ 01.03

FABIO Hi, Gabriela. Do you have five minutes?
GABRIELA Sure. What did you want to talk to me about?
F Well, I'm doing a triathlon next month. Didn't you read my post?
G No, I haven't seen it. A triathlon, wow! What for? That sounds really tough!
F Yeah, it's not easy. It's swimming, biking, then running.
G Which of those is the most difficult?
F All of them! Um, weren't you a good swimmer once?
G Yeah, once. What are you looking at me like that for?
F Do you think you could coach me?
G I don't know if I have enough time. Can I think about it and call you later?
F No problem. That's great! I'll swim a lot faster with your help.
G Who knows? You might win!

▶ 01.04

You don't need to get a very expensive camera. These have a lot of functions you just don't need. Do you know what I mean?
But whatever camera you buy, read the instructions carefully. Make sure you know what your camera can do. Did you get that?
When you take a photo, the most important thing is the light. Basically, the more light, the better, so choose the right time of day and place. Do you get the idea?
Always remember to keep still. If the camera moves, you get a bad photo.
Another thing to remember is to take your time. Only real professionals can take good photos in a hurry.
Is that clear? Do you want me to explain any of this again?

▶ 01.05

1 I must go and see her soon.
2 The nurse said I must eat less bread.
3 We've got to have more help.
4 Sorry, you can't take one with you.
5 Haven't any of the people arrived?
6 Sarah said she didn't do the homework.
7 Claudia has been there, hasn't she?
8 The store might open again.
9 We can't use our phones here.
10 The children must go first.

▶ 01.06

MICHAEL What are you reading?
SARAH An article about this guy … Frane … Selak.
M Who's that?
S He's a man from Croatia …. They've called him the unluckiest man in the world. It looks like he's had an incredible life.
M Incredible, how?
S Well, … It started in the 1960s. He says he was on a train that went off the tracks and crashed into a river – 17 people died, but he survived!
M Lucky.
S He did break his arm, though. Anyway, the next year he was flying on a small plane, which also crashed. The incredible thing was that as it was about to crash, one of the doors opened – the article says it had a fault – and he was sucked out. He landed safely, but nobody on the plane survived!
M That's amazing!
S I know. Then a few years later, he was in a bus accident. There was heavy rain, and the bus driver lost control on the wet roads and crashed into a river. He survived, although four people drowned. Then, he was in a car that caught fire while he was driving it on the highway. He managed to get out with seconds to spare before the gas tank exploded.
M Wow. I don't think I ever want to travel with this guy …
S Yeah, but that's not all …. He got hit by a bus in 1995.
M But he was OK?
S Of course. And then the year after, he had another car crash. He was driving on a road in the mountains, and he had to turn to avoid a truck coming in the other direction. So then his car went off the edge of the mountain and when it hit the bottom, it exploded. But Selak was OK because he'd managed to jump out just before it went over the edge. He was found holding onto a tree near the side of the road.
M That's just amazing.
S Yeah.
M But I don't know whether he's unlucky or extremely lucky.
S Well, the story's not finished yet. Apparently in 2003, he won the Croatian lottery – with the first ticket he'd ever bought.
M No way!
S That's what it says! So in the end, he's definitely lucky, not unlucky!
M Or maybe a mix of both.
S Yeah, maybe.
M Do you think all that's true? Can all these things really happen to one person?
S I don't know. I don't think everyone believes it. And it says there's no record of any plane crash in Croatia in the 1960s.
M Hmm.
S So I don't know. What do you think?
M Well, it's a fascinating story, so I want to believe it's true. But who knows?
S Yeah.
M What did he do with the lottery money, by the way?
S Well, first he bought himself a luxury home, that kind of thing. But then he decided to sell it and give most of the money away to friends and family because he thought that money couldn't buy happiness.
M Well, it could all be true then. Anyone who would give away all their lottery winnings must be a really good person, so they wouldn't make up a story like that. I think that's really inspiring.

UNIT 2

▶ 02.01

One evening many years ago, I was thinking about what to do when my friend Maria called. Maria was in a good mood because she had finished all her exams and was free now. She came over, and we decided to go for a walk. We hadn't gone very far when we saw something very unusual inside the old building near the market. Years earlier, the place burned down. No one knew how the fire had started, but ever since then, the place had been empty. Anyway, in one of the windows we saw a face, the face of a young girl. She obviously had been crying because there were still tears on her face. It was getting dark by then, but we could still see her clearly. "Did you see that?" I whispered to Maria. We had never been in this building before and felt a little scared, but we went inside to find the girl. She was wearing some really old clothes. They were dirty and smelled of smoke. "I didn't get out." she said, crying again. "I was too late!" We looked at each other and ran all the way home. The place is now a restaurant, and all our friends wonder why Maria and I will never go there with them!

▶ 02.02

1 We'd been swimming in the ocean.
2 Fishing had been fun, and I wanted to try it again.
3 I'm not sure what's been decided.
4 What had they been doing on their trip?
5 He's been told to rest at home.
6 Tim had been learning to ride a bike.
7 She'd never been climbing in her life.
8 Her husband's been worried about her.
9 The expedition had been my idea at first.
10 The TV reporters had been trying to interview him.

▶ 02.03

MARIO Hi, Silvia. Are you coming camping with us?
SILVIA If you still want me to, sure.
M Great. It should be a lot of fun unless the weather gets bad.
S As long as we get a couple of days of decent weather, I don't mind. What do I need to take?
M The usual stuff. When I get home, I'll text you the list I've made just in case. You don't need to worry about food, though. I've packed enough provided you like pasta. That's the easiest thing to make.
S Fine. In case we run out of pasta, I'll take some canned tuna and rice.
M Good idea. If you want, bring some cards. We could play at night.
S Sure. That'll be fun as long as I don't forget to pack them. Text me tomorrow as soon as you get up.
M OK. Remember to buy pepper spray because we might see bears.
S If I see a bear, I'll run all the way home!

▶ 02.04

MIKE It's a beautiful day!
LUCY It's great, isn't it? Why don't we go to the beach?
M Yes, let's go!
L We could drive but let's walk. We need the exercise.
M We do, don't we? I'll get my things.
L Last time you forgot your towel.
M That's right. I didn't have it with me, did I? Now I remember that I borrowed yours. Anyway, let's go.

…

L That was great, wasn't it? I'm really hungry now.
M Me too. This place looks good.
L Yeah, we've been here before, haven't we? They make really good pizza.
M That's right. Oh, I don't have my wallet. You couldn't lend me some money, could you?
L First a towel, then your wallet. You never remember anything, do you?
M Well, we're friends, aren't we? Come on, let's go inside.

▶ 02.05

1 **A** You're so good about recycling.
  B Do you think so?
2 **A** Your hair is amazing!
  B I'm glad you like it.
3 **A** You really managed to get it just right.
  B Guess it's not bad.
4 **A** The color is just perfect.
  B It's not bad, is it?
5 **A** It's so tasty!
  B It's all right.
6 **A** That was a wonderful present!
  B I'm glad you like it.

▶ 02.06

1 It was a great idea, wasn't it?
2 You don't know where Tustin Avenue is, do you?
3 That's obvious, isn't it?
4 They just didn't understand, did they?
5 He hasn't finished college yet, has he?
6 I'm not on the team, am I?
7 They will be able to do it, won't they?
8 You've been there before, haven't you?
9 She's forgotten all about it, hasn't she?
10 She's not going to agree, is she?

▶ 02.07

ANNOUNCER A woman reported missing over a month ago has been found safe. Camila Pérez, who works as an assistant chef, was expected home shortly after 9 p.m. Her family was not initially concerned because she had recently joined a gym and often went there after work before returning home. But when she still hadn't returned by early next morning, they contacted the police. Here's Michael Sanderson with the full report.

REPORTER When Camila Pérez went missing last month, it seemed like a complete mystery. Police knew she had left work by car after she finished her shift at 8:15 p.m., but after that, there were no signs of her at all. But last Saturday, the mystery was solved – Camila was found alive inside her car, under over a meter of snow, where she had managed to survive for 15 days. Police say there was no problem with her car, and that it seems she got into trouble when she decided, because of the heavy snow, to take a different route. But she didn't get very far – her car was found two kilometers from the main road. Police say she stopped soon after turning because the road was so bad but was unable to turn back. She then spent a night in the car expecting to be able to get home the next day, but the snow got heavier, and her car got totally stuck. Earlier, I spoke to Sergeant Granger, who gave us further details.

POLICE OFFICER We've only been able to speak very briefly to Camila at the hospital, so we don't know the full story yet. But it seems she turned on that road to try and avoid some of the snow on the main road, but obviously she didn't get anywhere and became stuck. Very few cars travel around this area during the winter unless there's some special reason, so she wasn't able to get anyone's attention to ask for help. So nobody saw her until yesterday, when a road maintenance crew went up there to check on the road conditions and saw the car under all the snow. When they found her, she was basically asleep. We could see she'd been eating in the car, that she had had some food in there, and she'd also been drinking melted snow. But it's incredible that she was able to survive with so little, really.

R Did they give you any idea at the hospital *how* she survived?

PO Well when she was found, her body temperature was very low and they think that because of the cold weather her body just kind of went to sleep, like some animals do in winter. She couldn't speak or walk when we found her. So the doctors say because her body basically went to sleep, she didn't need much food or water. But she was sure lucky.

R And do they think she's going to be OK?

PO They think so, yes – she's going to make a full recovery. She has a few problems now, but she should get over them fine.

R So, it's a story with a happy ending, fortunately. We'll give you more news on Camila's condition as soon as we get it.

UNIT 3

▶ 03.01

When I was in school, I didn't think I was good at anything. The other kids picked things up really quickly, but I didn't, and some kids looked down on me as some kind of loser. The only thing that I was interested in was cars, and I spent hours in the garage with my mom's old car, checking it out. My mom wasn't into cars at all though, and she was tired of me going on about them all the time. Anyway, one day there was a school trip. I woke up early to catch the bus. We were going down the road when the bus suddenly stopped. I thought we had run out of gas, but the driver told us there was an engine problem and he would have to call a mechanic. I went to see for myself and quickly figured out what to do: I just needed to put a cable back. After ten minutes, the bus was on the road again. After that, everyone looked up to me, and I realized there was something I could do well. When I finished school, I set up my own car repair business, and now I'm doing really well.

▶ 03.02

MARIANA Have you heard of this writer Daniel Kalder?
LIAM Yes, I read *Strange Telescopes* a while ago. It's an extraordinary book.
M I agree. Kalder has this ability to make a serious statement but make you laugh at the same time.
L It really is outstanding. I just wish I had some talent for writing.
M Kalder is successful because he spent so many years improving his style. That kind of hard work is exceptional.
L True. I don't think many people have heard of Kalder yet, but he has the potential to be a really well-known writer.
M He's very skilled at what he does, so I wish him all the best.

▶ 03.03

Shantelle Gaston-Hird has just broken a world record! Yesterday in Manchester, England, she ran a half-marathon – that's just over 21 kilometers – in 2 hours, 16 minutes, and 3 seconds. Shantelle is 32 years old, and this is the second time she has beaten all the best runners in the world. From March 2017 to January 2019, Shantelle held the world record, and now, just ten months later, she has set a new world record!

Shantelle started retro-running – running backward – for fun, but soon after, she began to take her hobby more seriously. But that's not all. She has also completed five marathons and eight ultra-marathons. It's safe to say that Shantelle has been running forward and backward for quite a while!

Every time she has raced, she has represented a charity. This time, Shantelle represented YoungMinds, a mental health charity for children and young people. She wants to show people that consistent training and determination can get extraordinary results.

▶ 03.04

Everyone thinks that professional athletes get paid a lot of money to compete, but this is not always true. The top athletes in smaller sports like handball, mountain running, and women's volleyball don't earn much money. Such sports are very competitive, and the athletes train hard, but even if they represent their country, they often can't make a living from their sport. Unfortunately, victory in championships and new world records very often don't mean money, especially if the sport isn't popular on TV. But maybe this doesn't matter if the athletes enjoy what they do, and spectators are happy to watch them perform and cheer for them. Money isn't everything, after all.

▶ 03.05

ELENA I know you like track and field, but do you ever take part in competitions?
DAVID Sometimes – in fact, I'm going to compete in the national championships next weekend.
E So you're almost a professional athlete then?
D Not really. It's hardly a profession, but I do a lot of training, and I'm hoping for a good performance. There'll be a lot of strong competitors, and I'll have to perform really well on the big day.
E So victory might be yours then, and we'll welcome the victorious champion home?
D Don't laugh, I might win!

▶ 03.06

1	game	came	6	save	safe
2	beach	peach	7	pie	buy
3	ferry	very	8	pig	pick
4	simple	symbol	9	pack	back
5	girl	curl	10	have a	have to

▶ 03.07

TINA Mark, I've been going through my closets, and I've found some old photos from school. Do you want to look at them?
MARK Yeah, of course!
T OK, well, here they are. There are a lot ... Look at this one – do you remember her? Martina?
M Oh yes, Martina ... I do. She was really good at math, and all those kinds of subjects, wasn't she?
T Yeah. I wonder what happened to her. She probably became an economist or something.
M Yeah, I'm sure. Anyway, I bet she's really successful, whatever she's doing.
T Oh, and here's one with you in it.
M Yeah, but who's that with me? I don't recognize her.
T That's Julia. Don't you remember her?
M Oh yeah, Julia, of course. She was really athletic, wasn't she?
T Yeah, she was good at tennis especially, I think.
M Well, I haven't seen her for years anyway.
T No. I know that she lives in Madrid now.
M Really?
T Yeah, she's been living there a while. I don't know what she's doing there, though.
M She wasn't my favorite person, to be honest. She was always a little too ... competitive.
T Yeah, I know what you mean. I wasn't good friends with her either. We ran track and field together, but she was always so arrogant. Like she thought she was better than us. And she was always going on about tennis!
M I wouldn't say she was arrogant, to be honest. Just too competitive for me!
T Hmm, look at this one. It's me, you, and Mr. Edwards.
M The best teacher ever!
T Hmm, I'm not sure about that.
M Come on! I thought he was exceptional. He was the only one that made me really feel I had any ability. You know what I was like in school. But he really seemed to believe in me.
T Well, I suppose what I liked was that he made us try out new things. But anyway ... take a look at this one.
M Oh, that's Sarah.
T Yeah. Didn't you fall out with her once? At a party or something?
M More than once, I think. We didn't get along – in fact, nobody at school got along with her.
T OK, let's move on quickly then! Here, look – it's our whole class, after a French class, isn't it?
M Yeah, look, there's the French teacher.
T Mrs. Taylor.
M Yep. That classroom doesn't bring back too many happy memories, I have to say.
T But you have a talent for languages. You speak French really well now, and Spanish.
M Yeah, but the lessons at school weren't for me. I'd say that Mrs. Taylor was skilled at teaching grammar, but we never did any kind of speaking practice, did we? I can only speak French because I've been to France so often and spoken to real French people.
T Hmm. Oh well, here's the last one. A school trip, but I don't know where we were.

M No, I don't either. That just looks like a field in the middle of nowhere! I used to love the school trips, though.

T Yeah, they were fun. And sometimes we even learned something!

M Sometimes, yeah. But most of the time it was just good to get out of school for a day!

UNIT 4

▶ 04.01

Richard Morgan lives on a boat in Chesapeake Bay in Virginia. His life used to be very different a few months ago. Richard graduated from law school in 2010 and got a great job at a law firm. It was interesting and paid well, but it was a very difficult job. Richard used to work 12 to 14 hours a day, and sometimes he would sleep at the office because it was so late. Richard realized that this kind of life was killing him. "I was used to spending all my time at work. It was normal for me – that was the frightening thing," Richard says. On Sundays, Richard would go for a walk along the bay, and he always enjoyed this. So one day, when he had had enough, he decided to change his life completely. He gave up his job, bought a boat, and said goodbye to his stressful life as a lawyer. "It was a big change, I still haven't gotten used to the ducks waking me up, but it's a great life," he says. "My family and friends were shocked at first, but now they are used to visiting me on my boat, and they know I'm happy."

▶ 04.02

KATE So what's it like to be a firefighter, Marco?

MARCO It's really tough, much harder than I thought. The training is very rigorous, and the instructors really stretch us.

K But you've finished all the training?

M Not yet. It's not so straightforward to become a firefighter. First, there's this arduous training schedule and then a tricky written test at the end.

K Well, you do like a challenge! It sounds like a very demanding job.

▶ 04.03

umbrella	attitude
pull	result
useless	influential
sugar	enthusiasm
supper	

▶ 04.04

BETO Education is getting worse and worse in this country.

LILY Oh, I don't know. Some things are improving.

B Like what? Teachers don't know what they're doing.

L I'm not sure about that. They work very hard.

B Yes, but they need more training.

L Maybe you're right, but teachers are not the real problem.

B True – kids just don't want to study.

L Really, do you think so?

B I do. They spend way too much time playing on their phones.

L I know what you mean, but on the other hand, technology is so important.

B Hang on, someone's texting me …

▶ 04.05

1 **A** It was an absolutely terrible hotel! I never want to go there again.
  B Oh, I don't know. It wasn't that bad.
2 **A** I really didn't like that movie. It was so boring!
  B Oh, I don't know. It wasn't that boring.
3 **A** I loved that restaurant. The menu was really original.
  B Oh, I don't know. It wasn't that original.
4 **A** Have you seen that new store? It looks great!
  B Oh, I don't know. It doesn't look that great.
5 **A** I thought the meeting today was way too long.
  B Oh, I don't know. It wasn't that long.

▶ 04.06

REPORTER I'm here on campus at the University of Seattle, on a day that many of the students here will remember for a long time – graduation day. I took the chance to speak to some of them today about this – you could maybe call it a life-changing day.
OK, so I'm here with Mateo. How are you feeling today?

MATEO Pretty happy! It hasn't been easy. I had to work really hard this past year, a lot of studying, a lot of time spent at the library or in my room with a pile of books in front of me. It was all pretty grueling really.

R Was it worth it?

M Oh, yeah, definitely. I feel great today. All the hard work paid off, I guess. It's really been a struggle at times – I'm a full-time student, or I was, but I also had to work in a restaurant for 20 hours a week to pay for my studies. So it was a challenge sometimes. But today, being here with my family and getting my diploma – it's great, and it's why I put in all that effort.

R Great, well, congratulations!

M Thank you.

R So, Samantha, are you happy today?

SAMANTHA Of course! It means I've finished college, and now I can go and find a job!

R So how has it been? It must have been a lot of work for you to get through.

S Well, yeah, I suppose. It's been tricky sometimes, but it's never been a struggle. I found most parts of my classes really straightforward. I always did pretty well on my exams, so it wasn't a big problem really. The only thing was that I had to take my last three final exams in two days – that was very demanding. But in the end, you just do it – you're forced to really. There's no choice.

R Enjoy your day.

S Thanks.

R OK, so we're going to speak to Luke. How are you feeling?

LUKE OK, I guess. Yeah, pretty good.

R You're not happy that you're graduating today?

L Yeah, I am happy, but I'm a little disappointed, too. I didn't get the grade I was hoping for, so today, well I'm happy, but I'm also a little bit … sad and disappointed, I guess.

R Sorry to hear that. Do you want to tell us what went wrong?

L I don't know really. On my last two exams, I just didn't get very good grades, and that influenced my final grades for those classes. I had a really bad cold the week before those last two final exams, so I think that affected me a little. But unless you're really sick on the day of the exam itself, the university doesn't take things like that into account. I don't think it's right because it probably had an effect on my performance.

R Well, I hope you enjoy your day despite your disappointment.

L Thanks.

R So, Jane, how are you feeling right now?

JANE I feel great! And relieved! It means I can relax a little.

R What kinds of things will you remember about your time in college?

J Mainly being tired, I think! It's been a pretty exhausting time. As you can probably tell, I'm a little older than most of the students graduating today. I was 40 when I decided to go to college. None of my friends or family had ever gone to college, so that really stretched me and challenged me. But that's also why I wanted to do it.

R And what's the future for you now? Have you found a job yet?

J Well, I already had a job – I never gave it up. But I hope having a degree opens up some more opportunities for me at work. I was kind of stuck before, I think.

R Thanks, and best of luck.

J Thanks.

UNIT 5

▶ 05.01

KATY Have you read this article, Josh? It says there's a good chance the next generation will live to be 150 years old!

JOSH Who knows, what it says may be true. But what evidence is there?

K Advances in medicine will certainly be a factor, and people won't die from all kinds of diseases common today. Also, technology will probably make everyday life easier.

J Fine, but I doubt if many people will want to live that long. It's unlikely that it'll be much fun to be 150.

K The article says that we will probably be able to work until that age. There's a good chance that machines will do all the hard work, such as washing and cleaning, so that we can do different tasks, such as critical thinking.

J Interesting. I'm sure there'll even be a special Olympics for people over 100!

K Yes, it's bound to happen, so start training!

▶ 05.02

/θ/	/ð/
think	breathing
athletic	mother
breath	either
Earth	leather
length	the
month	though

▶ 05.03

Let's travel to the year 2059! We won't be living on Earth because pollution and wars will have destroyed the old planet. Instead, planet Zeus will be our home. Giant spaceships will have transported everyone and everything from Earth before it exploded in 2055. Zeus won't be a bad place to live and some things will go on as normal. Adults will be going to work every morning. Children will be studying in school, and old people will be complaining about almost everything. Many things will be different, though. Because of the different atmosphere, our hair will have turned green – at least it won't have fallen out – and we will be walking around in space suits. Special pills will have replaced food and drink, so we won't be cooking at all and we won't be eating out at restaurants. Yes, life will have changed a lot.
Welcome to 2059, and the future we will have created.

▶ 05.04

MAGDA You know, I'm seriously thinking of taking this job in Paris.

PABLO You should! One good thing is the higher salary. It's basically a promotion.

M True, but the trouble with that is more pressure and stress. A big disadvantage of the position I've been offered is that I'll have too much to do.

P Come on, one of the best things about you is how you respond to a challenge.

M I guess so … Another problem with this job offer is that I'll need to improve my French – and fast!

P No need to worry about that either. The advantage of living and working in a foreign country is that you learn the language quickly.

M You have an answer for everything!

P The only drawback of the job I can see is the size of the company. Do you really want to work in a company that big?

M If they pay me enough money, yes!

▶ 05.05

A How about eating out tonight for a change?

B It's an idea, I suppose. Where should we go?

A There's a new Thai place that just opened.

B Hmm, I don't know about that. I'm not in the mood for spicy food.

A Well, there's the Italian place just up the hill.

B That might be worth a try, and it's not far.

A Let's walk there. It's a beautiful day.

B Yes, that makes sense. I need the exercise!

A We could invite Amelia and Rob, too.

B That's not a bad idea. They'd need to drive there, though.

A Then they could give us a ride if we feel too lazy to walk back.
B That's a possibility, although we might have to invite them in for coffee or something.
A So I have an excuse to make one of your favorite lemon cakes.
B That's a great idea! I can't remember the last time you made one.

▶ **05.06**
1 The trouble is it could take a long time to get the money.
2 The good thing is we're not far from downtown.
3 The problem is people are starting to talk about her.
4 The advantage is the price isn't very high.
5 The drawback is no one really knows what's going to happen.
6 The advantage is we can see a lot more of each other.
7 The trouble is I'm not sure I have time to help him.
8 A disadvantage is it means selling the car.

▶ **05.07**
ANDREW What are you reading, Carla?
CARLA It's just an article about a supermarket chain. It has most of the products that a normal supermarket has, but it doesn't sell anything with packaging – so nothing's sealed in plastic, not fruit, not vegetables, not even meat or eggs.
A Really? How does that work?
C Well, you just bring your own bags, or boxes, or whatever.
A Oh, I see ... Isn't that a little complicated?
C Or you can get bags there. But then you bring them back and use them again and again.
A Well, I guess it sounds like a good idea. But I don't think I'll be going to a supermarket like that by choice.
C Why not?
A Well, when I go shopping I just want to get everything done quickly. I don't want to have to worry about bringing my own boxes or packing things myself.
C But it's much more environmentally friendly!
A Sure, I imagine it is, but I'm too busy for that kind of thing. And anyway, I already do a lot. I'm aware that we have to think about climate change, so I don't use the car too much, I try to recycle, I turn the water off when I'm brushing my teeth, that kind of thing.
C I really don't think that taking some extra bags to the supermarket is going to take you that much time! Just think of all the damage that's caused by plastic packaging. Producing it pollutes Earth's atmosphere, and that's the kind of thing that causes climate change.
A Well, ...
C But it's not just that – it has a big impact in general. A lot of packaging ends up in the ocean, in rivers ...
A I know. You're probably right. I guess I'm just lazy.
C Well, I know it's not easy. But there are lots of things I think we could all do to reduce our carbon footprint ...
A Like what?
C Well, only taking public transportation, for example. Never using the car.
A Not easy.
C I know, but there's a difference between "not easy" and "impossible." Or we could all become vegetarian.
A Does that help the environment?
C Yes, because producing meat uses a lot of energy and water, much more than producing vegetables.
A Does it? Oh. I had no idea.
C And it takes up more space, too. More land, I mean, to farm all those big cows ...
A Well, I guess that could be a good reason to cut down on meat. But do you really think people are going to be happy to change their lifestyles like this?
C No, that's my point. We could all do more, but we don't. We just talk about what we should do.
A Personally, I think there's a chance that technology will save us. You know, if we're able to come up with technology that doesn't harm the environment, factories that don't pollute the air, really efficient machines that don't use much energy ...

C Yeah, there's always that hope, but I think we'll have destroyed the planet before we manage to come up with smart enough technology.
A I guess we'll see. I'm not as pessimistic as you, though.
C Well, one thing's for sure – if we don't start to deal with the problem, then people on this planet will be paying for it for a long time.

UNIT 6

▶ **06.01**
ELENA Hi, Max, good to see you. How's your summer?
MAX Boring! I'm looking forward to going back to college. Sitting in front of the computer all day is not my idea of a vacation.
E Why don't you go somewhere to take a break? I think it's really important to get away from everything once in a while.
M Traveling is a waste of time. I remember visiting Paris last spring. I tried to see the *Mona Lisa* in the Louvre, but there were so many people, I couldn't even get in the room, which was just as well since I'd forgotten to take my camera. Anyway, I'm not interested in walking around in crowds of tourists.
E Sorry to hear that – but look, stop being so negative. You obviously like art – that's why you went to the Louvre – so why not do something connected with that? I can see you doing something creative.
M I've tried painting and I wasn't too bad at it.
E There you go. You may go on to be in the Louvre yourself one day!

▶ **06.02**
Welcome to Niagara Falls! This is your personal audio guidebook. Remember to turn the volume up high because it's pretty noisy here. You can hear the water pouring down the falls, millions of liters every minute. If you want to admire the view, press the red button to stop the guide, and then the blue button to continue and go on listening. It's amazing to think that the falls have been here for 10,000 years. Basically, ice melting into the Niagara River made it powerful enough to cut a huge piece out of the rock. More about this later. Back to today: millions of tourists come to visit the falls every year. Having so many visitors is great, but all the activity causes a lot of damage, so we are trying to protect the falls as much as possible. So ...

▶ **06.03**
The Palomar Hotel is located in a perfect setting on the outskirts of Phoenix just half an hour away from downtown and minutes from the hiking trails going up into the Phoenix Mountains. It's an ideal conference venue with a number of features delegates will appreciate. Whether you're outside relaxing on the patio admiring the views over coffee, or inside in the lobby bar, you'll feel completely at home. In fact, why not book a studio apartment so that it really is a home away from home?

▶ **06.04**
a We had some superb meals at an excellent local restaurant.
b These ideas are a big contrast to what we heard yesterday.
c The Pyramids in Egypt are the most impressive structures I've ever seen.
d Their discussion lasted two hours.
e We can't destroy the original document.
f The train terminal is a short walk from the airport.

▶ **06.05**
Speak any language in 30 days! That's right, with our new online course, any language can be learned effortlessly. This is made possible by an amazing piece of software that is being used today by thousands of people studying 25 different languages in the comfort of their own homes.
It's so simple. All the work is done online, and the course is complete. No expensive extras have to be bought. But don't listen to us; listen to our customers:

"I was promoted back in January, but I needed to improve my English. This course had been recommended to me by a coworker, so I bought it and the results were amazing! Now I am being considered for an overseas position, and I'm hoping my salary will be increased."
"I have been given a completely new direction in life by this course. Now I can communicate with people all over the world. I'm so glad I was persuaded to sign up."
What are you waiting for? Send us an email and you will be contacted by our customer care team within 24 hours. Goodbye! ¡Adios! Poka! Ciao!

▶ **06.06**
A Professor, why is it important to keep languages alive?
B Because the survival of languages means the preservation of cultures, too.
A Are many languages being lost?
B You can see the disappearance of smaller languages all the time.
A Can you give any examples?
B Belorussian, the language in Belarus, hasn't died out, but it is in decline and future generations might not speak it at all.
A What about the opposite?
B There has been a revival of Cornish, a Celtic language.
A But what causes language loss?
B Basically, competition with bigger languages. The increase in English as a major international language is a massive factor. The effect goes beyond just language.
A What do you mean?
B Well, globalization can also mean a deterioration in local customs.
A That sounds depressingly true.

▶ **06.07**
1 **A** I hope you don't mind my asking, but are you around this weekend?
  B Yes, I am. Do you need a favor?
2 **A** Hi, Rosie. There's an idea I'd like to run past you.
  B What's that?
3 **A** I was wondering if you wouldn't mind helping me with something?
  B No, not at all. What is it?
4 **A** Great! I don't know how to thank you.
  B Oh, don't worry about it.
5 **A** Do you mind if I ask you to get my coat?
  B No problem, where is it?
6 **A** I'm really sorry to ask you this, but could you give me a ride home?
  B Sure, let's go.

▶ **06.08**
MARION Good to see you, Derek! Do you mind if I ask you something?
DEREK No, not at all. Go right ahead.
M I hope you don't mind my asking, but I was wondering if you wouldn't mind writing a few words for the club website? We're trying to get members' profiles on there.
D Sure, that sounds good. I'm happy to help. Just tell me what kind of thing you'd like.
M Super, I really appreciate it.
D It's no trouble at all.

▶ **06.09**
1 I'm not sure people watch as much television as they used to.
2 She's also the author of a collection of children's books.
3 The damage to our fragile environment has several causes.
4 I never got to know her niece very well, though.
5 The report suggests taking a fresh look at the healthcare system.
6 It's an adventure story that starts with the main character in prison.
7 There was a lot of confusion and embarrassment when I asked the question.
8 I do appreciate how urgent this matter has become.
9 **A** Thanks anyway for checking.
  B It's my pleasure.
10 Occasionally, I have a dessert after dinner as a treat.

▶ 06.10

PRESENTER Hello, and welcome to this week's travel podcast. As you know, we normally like to invite listeners on to talk about faraway places they've visited, but this week it's almost the opposite – we're talking about staycations. If you don't know what they are, well, the word "staycation" is a combination of "stay" and "vacation," and it's basically a vacation that you take in your own home, or at least staying at your own home at night. Why do that? Well, for economic reasons, to avoid the stress of traveling, to explore your local area, and even to enjoy your own house a little. Now, we have three people to talk to us about their staycations. So let's speak first to Mike and hear about his … well, I won't say trip because you didn't go anywhere.

MIKE No, I didn't!

P But tell us about it anyway!

M Yes, well, I had a four-day staycation last week. I took Friday and Monday off work – my wife did too – so we had four days in all.

P And what did you do?

M Well, we'd planned a lot, so we knew there was a concert we wanted to go to on the Saturday night, and a photo exhibition as well. We also took a day trip to the coast and spent the day by the ocean.

P Sounds nice.

M It was. But those are things we'd do anyway, on the weekend. I think it was the little things we did differently that made the experience interesting. So, every morning, we had a big breakfast together, like in a hotel. Normally, we just eat a bowl of cereal, generally not at the same time, but this time we prepared fresh fruit, had yogurt, something hot like eggs or toast, that kind of thing. It was great to sit together and really enjoy it.

P OK.

M And also we had made some rules. No TV. No Internet. No checking emails. So we did different things – we read a lot. We listened to music. I even did some painting, and my wife wrote some poetry.

P Oh, wow. OK, now let's talk to our second guest. Samantha, tell us about your staycation.

SAMANTHA Well, I wanted it to be active, like an exercise vacation. So I planned everything around that idea. I tried to do something active every day. So one day I went running in the countryside, another day I went biking, then I went for a walk.

P Sounds tiring.

S It was, and actually on the last day, I gave up and stayed home and slept! The other thing I did was to treat myself to takeout every other day. I felt I'd earned it with all that physical activity!

P Well, thanks. Now, finally, let's hear from Lily. What did you get up to?

LILY Well, my experience was more of a challenge because, unlike the other two, I have two kids to entertain!

P Right, so what did you do to keep them busy?

L Well, kind of like the others, I tried to find an activity every day. So we took a trip to the zoo, we went to see a soccer game, went out for lunch to a restaurant, we all cooked together at home, and we went to a concert. I tried to have the same rule as Mike – no TV or Internet – but that was too hard with kids. They couldn't understand why we'd want to change. But overall, it went pretty well. I think it felt different for the kids compared to just staying at home while on school break. They felt we were all doing something different.

P OK, thanks, Lily. So, as usual, I'll ask you all for a score out of ten and whether you'd recommend a staycation to our listeners. So first, Lily.

L I'd give it seven out of ten. It's not easy with kids, but it's worth a try.

P Thanks. Samantha?

S Eight out of ten. I'd recommend it, but it's probably better to have more variation instead of doing exercise every single day!

P OK, and Mike?

M I really enjoyed it. You have to make an effort, but if you do, I think it's a great way to spend a few days. So nine out of ten, and yes, I'd definitely recommend doing what I did.

UNIT 7

▶ 07.01

Sleep debt means you don't get enough sleep. The causes are obvious – too much work and not enough rest basically – but what are the symptoms? Well, do you ever feel so tired in the middle of the day that you can't keep your eyes open? Do you ever get such bad headaches that you have to lie down for a while? Does this sound like you? If so, you need to do something about it. Actually, you don't need much sleep to recover from the day, but you should make sure you get enough rest – at least seven hours each day. In fact, too much sleep, more than nine hours, can be as bad as too little sleep, six hours or less. It is a good idea to take an afternoon nap, a siesta, especially if you can't get enough hours during the night. Some people say they feel so refreshed after a nap that they can do twice as much. By the way, don't try not to sleep at all – people have died after too many days without sleep. Take my advice and go to bed right away!

▶ 07.02

There is a lot of criticism of big cities, and in many ways, they are soft targets. When you're driving through a major city, the traffic congestion gives you a lot of time to think, as does the time spent looking for a parking space. You should consider the option of living in a small town. There you would really need your car because public transportation is almost non-existent outside major residential areas, and nearly everything, such as the kids' schools or the supermarket, would be a drive away. Let's hope you get along well with the local residents because you'll be seeing a lot of the same faces in the same places. Of course, with all that fresh air, the quality of life must be better, but at the same time, you'll miss all the sights and sounds of the big city. It makes you think, doesn't it? So, roll down your window, breathe in that air pollution, and be grateful for urban development.

▶ 07.03

Park Hospital, the best drama series on TV, returns Monday with the first episode of season five. For those of you who don't know, here's some background: Park Hospital witnessed the good and the bad of New York City in the 1970s and '80s – its brave doctors and nurses confronted some of the city's worst crime and disease. Their stories are now captured on screen with a script written by screenwriter Ben Goldberg and a cast of household names. The stories come to life against beautiful shots of New York City and the original Park Hospital. And *Park Hospital* is now broadcast all over the world. In fact, the first four seasons were recently released on many international streaming services. To make this show appropriate for all ages, some scenes were cut by our editors because they dealt with topics that not all viewers may be ready for. We want the whole family to watch! So on Monday, when you hear that familiar soundtrack come on, make sure you join us to watch the best drama on TV.

▶ 07.04

Anne Boleyn was the second wife of Henry VIII. She was executed in 1536 to make way for Henry's new love, Jane Seymour, whom Henry married shortly after Anne's execution. Anne obviously didn't take this too well, and in fact, there have been regular reports of people seeing Anne's ghost. Perhaps the most famous incident was at the Tower of London, where poor Anne was executed. In 1864, a soldier saw Anne and shouted at her to stop. Anne didn't and so the soldier walked right through her. The shock made him pass out.

▶ 07.05

1 Local residents are getting worried about the crime rate.
2 There's a new shopping mall just outside of town.
3 She said the living room was cozy, but really, it was just small.
4 Everyone should know the threat of climate change by now.
5 The police officers are working closely with the local community.

6 We put a solar panel on the roof to cut energy costs.
7 Disneyland is probably the best-known amusement park.
8 You can never find a parking space when you need one.
9 Pour it down the kitchen sink if you don't want it.
10 More could be done to help developing nations and build a better educational system.

▶ 07.06

JULIE Hi Sam, sorry I'm late.
SAM That's OK, Julie. Everything OK?
J Yeah, you know, just the usual – couldn't find a parking space. There just aren't enough around here.
S Yeah, I know.
J I would've used public transportation, but it probably would've taken even longer. The buses from where I work take such a long time to get downtown. There's so much traffic congestion on the roads there.
S Yeah, I suppose I'm lucky I live so close to downtown. But sometimes I do get tired of it, to be honest.
J Really?
S Yeah, well, I think the quality of life where you live is probably better. There's so much air pollution here in downtown, and then all the traffic congestion … well, you know about that.
J Yes, I certainly do.
S Sometimes I think it would be nice to live in a nice residential area like you do, instead of downtown. In a big house instead of my apartment!
J Well, there are definitely advantages. I can take the subway to downtown from where I live, and it's really fast and convenient.
S Yeah, exactly.
J But there isn't much for local residents, really. I mean, there are just apartments and houses where I live, and a few supermarkets. No movie theaters, no museums. You have all the entertainment you could want right at your doorstep.
S Yeah, I know – I'm lucky in a lot of ways. And if I want to get something done, it's normally pretty easy – I don't have to travel too far.
J Yeah, and to be honest, I'm not sure if the air quality is much better where I live than downtown. I mean, it's still the same city, right?
S Maybe, but at least you have some greenery to help. I'm sure that sucks in some of the pollution. Downtown there's what – one park?
J Hmm … two.
S Oh, yeah, two. You see – I never go to the parks here. They're not very nice. There are people there that I don't really feel comfortable sitting next to on a bench.
J No, I agree – we have some nice parks where I live. But you have your big balcony. You have some plants and flowers out there.
S Yeah, but it's not the same.
J I know, but remember what they say – the grass is always greener on the other side of the fence. You live downtown, and you dream about living where I do. And sometimes I really wish I still lived downtown!
S Really?
J Of course. Just to be in the middle of everything again. But I'm sure I'd get sick of it.
S The thing is, I don't think things used to be so bad. There are so many more cars now than ten years ago. So many more people, I think.
J Yeah.
S And life just gets faster and faster. People don't know when to slow down anymore. Living downtown feels like living at double the speed of the rest of the world.
J Maybe, but it's not too different for people who commute in, you know. Everyone hurries onto the train, hurries off, hurries to the office, hurries back home.
S Yeah, but in the evening, you can relax.

J Hardly. Most evenings I just think about all the work I have to do the next day!
S Oh, it can't be that bad.
J No, I'm exaggerating. I do manage to relax in the evening.
S Me too. We should both stop complaining – I'm sure there are a lot of people who'd love to live where we do.
J You're right. Let's go and get some coffee …

UNIT 8

▶ **08.01**

1 If I stop eating out, I'll save a lot of money.
2 If I didn't need to work, I'd become a full-time writer.
3 If I see Jim, I'll return the $20 I owe him.
4 If the bank didn't charge such high interest, I'd take out a bigger loan.
5 If the price is too high, I won't buy the apartment.
6 If Sarah paid back her student loan any time soon, I'd be surprised.
7 If I feel generous, I might give some money to charity.
8 If I were you, I'd think about what I was doing.
9 If I worked for myself, I could have more responsibility.
10 If we spend more on advertising, profits can increase.

▶ **08.02**

John Roberts made a living as a fisherman working for a big fishing company. However, John always wanted to have his own boat and business, so he put aside savings for years, and when the interest rate was low, he went to a bank. The bank checked the budget that John had prepared showing sales versus costs and then agreed to finance the project. This meant John now had a very large debt, but he considered the boat a sound investment. Unfortunately, business became more difficult because of overfishing and environmental damage. John's income dropped lower and lower, and he was struggling just to pay off the interest on his loan. Before long, the bank was starting to charge him penalties for missed payments. John was desperate, and he wrote about his situation on a website for start-up companies. This worked. The local council immediately awarded John a grant and donations came in from people in the area. Thanks to this, John's business survived.

▶ **08.03**

One night, I came home very late and couldn't find my keys, so I had to break into my own house! I was climbing through a window when a woman on the street shouted, "Police! There's a burglary!" I got down and explained that it was my house and I wasn't a burglar, but she called me a liar. She said that she was a witness and that she would give evidence when I was accused of breaking and entering. She would happily come to the trial in court to testify against me. She was really excited now and went on to say that the jury would find me guilty, and the judge would give me a very long prison sentence. I'd have to go to a horrible prison where the prisoners murder one another and steal their cellmates' food just to survive. She was out of breath now and just about to start again when suddenly my house keys fell out of my back pocket. I wished her goodnight and went inside my house.

▶ **08.04**

1 It should have been sent on Tuesday.
2 If I had seen her, I would have shouted.
3 If you had told me, it could have been different.
4 We'd never have known if she had stayed home.
5 They shouldn't have thrown it away.
6 She shouldn't have taken my purse.

▶ **08.05**

1 **A** We'll never be able to afford it.
  B Don't give up hope.
2 **A** I'll never see her again.
  B I'm sure you will.

3 **A** It started to go wrong right from the start.
  B It might work out fine.
4 **A** That's another opportunity lost.
  B There'll be plenty more, don't worry.
5 **A** I'm really worried about this interview.
  B I'm sure it'll be fine.
6 **A** There's not much chance of it working.
  B You never know. We might pull it off.

▶ **08.06**

I'm really sorry to hear about your car. The same thing happened to me a couple of years ago. My car was stolen right outside my house, and believe it or not, I just had a similar experience, I had my wallet stolen from my purse when I was in line at the supermarket. That doesn't surprise me. It was just like that when I called the insurance company. They kept me waiting for ages, so I know the feeling. It was the same with me. What can you do? True, that's just like when Sarah's apartment was robbed. I don't know what things are coming to.

▶ **08.07**

1 Hello, this is John Peters.
2 It's Simon again from National Bank.
3 It's 973-4124.
4 No, but thanks anyway.
5 Do you want to pay by cash or by credit card?
6 That's fine, no worries.
7 I'm sorry, but I didn't get that.
8 All the best and speak to you soon.
9 Bye, thanks for calling.

▶ **08.08**

PRESENTER Hello, and welcome to this week's *Crime View*, where we ask you for help in solving crimes in the local area. As always, you can call us on our toll-free phone number and the information you give will go directly to the police. You don't have to leave your name, and any information you give could lead to a cash reward. So, let's go to our first crime. Monica Leonard has the details.
MONICA Our first report is about an incident that happened at the Highlands Shopping Mall. Two weeks ago, a man walked into one of the jewelry stores here. He talked to the assistant and asked to see a number of different watches. While all this was going on, a second man entered. He appeared to look at some bracelets and other jewelry, and then he left. But soon after, staff realized that over $2,000 worth of jewelry had been taken by the second man. The men are described as being in their early thirties, both with dark hair. The second man had blue glasses.
P Thank you, Monica. Police would like to hear from anyone who has information about this. If anyone has tried to sell you jewelry on the street, in cafés, or anywhere else, please reach out. Now let's hear from Steven Craven about another crime the police need your help with.
STEVEN Well, at General Electronics store on Park Road three days ago, a young man was seen running out into the parking lot with a bag full of items taken from the store. The items included headphones, smartphones, tablets, and a number of other expensive things. One young woman, a local student, tried to stop him after she realized that staff from the store were shouting at him. The man accidentally knocked her over as he ran past. The woman wasn't hurt, but the thief managed to escape. The young woman said she didn't see the man's face clearly because it was too dark, but that he was wearing blue jeans and a red T-shirt.
P Thank you, Steven. If you think you might know who the thief was, please get in touch. Now, we're joined in the studio by Detective Hugo Ramirez, who is going to tell us about a series of crimes that have occurred over the last month or so.
DETECTIVE RAMIREZ Yes, thank you. Over the last six weeks, we've unfortunately seen thieves break into six different houses at night and steal a number of things. All these incidents have happened in a pretty small area – mainly in the

area between Thatch Road and Crescent Drive. It's mainly jewelry that has been stolen. In each case, the thieves involved were able to enter the houses through open windows. Now, I realize that in this hot weather nobody wants to keep their windows closed, but we think that most of these crimes wouldn't have happened if the owners of the houses had made sure to close all their windows before going to bed. So, please get in touch if you have any information, but also – please make sure you close your windows before going to bed, or if you're going out.
P Thank you, Detective Ramirez. We'd like to finish with an update on one of the crimes featured on a previous show. Well, last month police caught two men accused of robbing the Newport Road gas station back in February. They appeared in court, were found guilty, and are now in prison. The names of the men involved were given directly to the police as a result of our show. So thanks again for your help – if we hadn't received your calls, that crime would not have been solved. So please call in with any information you might have about the stories we've covered tonight. Together, we're keeping our community safer.

UNIT 9

▶ **09.01**

We like to think that we live in a world where everyone has access to professional medical care that can take care of their needs. Unfortunately, for those who live in the developing world, which is about 85% of Earth's population, this is far from the case. Too often either the treatment from trained professionals that they need is impossible to get, or it costs money that they don't have. People who need treatment then often have to look for alternatives that are relatively cheap and available.
There is a long tradition of using natural medicine, such as plants whose leaves and flowers can be used to take away pain. However, natural medicine is of limited use in situations where the patient is very sick. Even so, there are people who suffer from serious diseases and who trust natural medicine more than modern methods. This may sound crazy to Westerners who have the luxury of professional help, but people that believe in this kind of treatment strongly enough might benefit just from the psychological effect, which could mean the difference between life and death.

▶ **09.02**

It all started when I was jogging in the park. I bumped into something, fell down, and got a big bruise on my leg. It ached a little. I was worried I had strained my leg because I couldn't walk comfortably. I thought it was best to do something about it, so I looked up some advice online and decided to treat myself.
There was a lot of information, all pretty confusing, but I found a recipe for a special sports drink and drank a couple of liters of it. About an hour later, it hit me. I felt dizzy, my head was spinning, and I started to shiver – I couldn't hold a cup in my hands. I thought I was going to pass out, but I managed to crawl into bed. A week later, I'm beginning to get over it, and thank goodness I didn't develop any complications. I won't be using any of those websites again, though.

▶ **09.03**

1 You have a terrible bruise on your leg!
2 Please be quiet so I can hear the TV.
3 The bodybuilder strained a muscle while he was working out.
4 This flu is a real nuisance – I can't do anything!
5 Eat plenty of fruit and vegetables to stay healthy.
6 I really like my scar – I think it suits me, and it makes me look more interesting.
7 I still feel guilty for not taking better care of her.
8 May I inquire how my wife is doing, Doctor?
9 All employees are required to attend the weekly meeting on Friday morning.

▶ 09.04

Simon Robins was a hero when he walked around the world to raise money for charity, but journalists have now discovered that he didn't do it. Actually, Robins flew most of the way. Journalists wondered how he had done the walk so quickly and asked him to explain. At first, Robins refused to talk about it, complaining that the press wanted to get a good story, and he completely denied having anything to hide. However, journalists found out he had used a private plane, and finally Robins admitted flying for part of the long trip. Robins insisted he had walked a lot of the way and promised to give money back to people who believed they had been cheated. The police have informed us that they won't be taking legal action against Robins, but they have ordered him to give a full and correct account of his "walk" around the world.

▶ 09.05

A Hi! Do you recognize me?
B Sorry, but I have no idea who you are.
A It's Tim, from Black Street.
B Black Street? I don't have a clue where that is.
A Oh, come on! Black Street, you must remember.
B I really have no idea. What in the world are you talking about?
A The Black Street Café. We worked there one summer.
B Oh, Tim! What in the world are you doing here?
A I wanted to ask you the same question.

▶ 09.06

A Here's your room. Have a nice stay.
B Umm, I understood that we booked a large room.
A It is large – you should see the small rooms.
B And did I get this wrong? I thought there was an ocean view.
A There's a nice painting of the ocean on the wall.
B There isn't even a shower!
A Have I misunderstood something? I thought you were on vacation. You'll be outside most of the time.
B But didn't you say this was a luxury hotel?
A It used to be – 20 years ago!

▶ 09.07

1 I met John downtown the other day.
2 Do you know where I could find a post office?
3 I can't afford it. It's too expensive.
4 That's Ben calling. Could you ask him where he is?
5 Don't leave the window open when you go out.
6 Can you play a song for us on the piano?
7 Don't assume I earn a lot of money doing this.
8 Where are you going? Come back here!
9 If it's so important to you, you can have mine.
10 I do think she ought to explain exactly what she did.

▶ 09.08

DOCTOR Good morning.
PATIENT Good morning, Doctor.
D Take a seat. What seems to be the trouble?
P Well, it's a number of things, actually. First, I think it's probably just a cold, but I wanted to check with you. Basically, I have a really bad cough. And I sneeze a lot.
D OK. So, how long have you had this cough?
P I'd say … I guess it's four days now. It's been worse for the last two days.
D OK.
P But I've had a sore throat a few times in the last few weeks.
D And have you had a fever at all?
P No.
D Any aches or pains in your body?
P No.

D Well, it's probably just a cold then. Get plenty of rest, and make sure you drink lots of liquid. You'll probably get over it in a few days without having to take anything.
P OK.
D Are you taking any painkillers?
P Yes, aspirin.
D Well that's OK. That'll help the sore throat.
P What I don't understand is why I keep getting sick. This is probably the third time I've come down with a cold in the last month. It seems strange.
D Well, it can happen. There are different cold viruses, and just when your body finishes fighting one, you can catch another one. It's normal at this time of year, so it's nothing to worry about.
P OK.
D But if the cough doesn't go away this time, let's say after a week, then come back and we'll give you a check to make sure you don't have a chest infection. But for now, it's nothing to worry about.
P OK. Umm, the other thing is that I had an accident yesterday while I was on my bike.
D Yes?
P I was biking down a hill in the forest, and I don't know what happened, but I fell off. And I hurt my arm and my side, here. I have a few bruises and it aches a little. I just wanted to check that everything was OK.
D OK, well, hmm … let me just ask first – did you hit your head at all when you fell?
P A little bit, yes.
D And did you lose consciousness?
P No, no, nothing like that. I was wearing a helmet, so I just felt a little dizzy. But I didn't feel like I was going to pass out or anything.
D Well, in any case, I think you really should have gone to the hospital to get yourself checked out if you bumped your head. Especially if you felt dizzy afterward.
P Oh, OK.
D Can I just see where you have these bruises?
P Yeah, sure.
D OK … Well … Let me just feel here … Does it hurt if I do this?
P No, not really.
D OK, well yes, I think you just have a few bruises. Your shoulder will probably ache for a while, and I think it's best if you stay off the bike for a few weeks at least.
P Oh, really? I'm supposed to be taking part in a race next week.
D Well, I wouldn't recommend that. Some gentle exercise is fine, but nothing like a race. You need to let your body get over the fall. Let me just see here … ooh, that's a pretty bad cut.
P Yeah, it hurts a little there.
D I'm going to give you a cream to treat that with. It will help it heal and it will stop you from getting any kind of infection there.
P OK.
D Here you are. Put it on three times a day.
P Can I just ask one more thing?
D OK, but it will have to be very quick because I have to move on to the next patient.
P Sure. I'm going on vacation in a couple of months to Cambodia. I wanted to know about any shots, that kind of thing.
D Well they can give you the information you need about that at reception. You'll need to make an appointment with one of our nurses here to get that done.
P OK.
D But speak to reception about it. They'll tell you everything you need to know.
P OK, thanks very much.
D Have a nice day.

UNIT 10

▶ 10.01

Shergar was a very successful champion racehorse; in fact, he might have been the best ever. His racing career ended in 1981, but he could have made his owners a lot more money if he hadn't been stolen in 1983. Shergar was never seen again.
There are lots of theories about who took Shergar and what happened to him, but in reality, anything may have happened. The kidnappers must have been very professional, or very lucky, because they hid their victim so successfully. It couldn't have been easy to steal such a famous horse and make it disappear completely. People say the police may not have done the best job looking for the horse because they could have acted a lot more quickly – but the truth is, they didn't have much evidence, and the horse and its kidnappers were never found.
Some people say the kidnappers must have killed Shergar when the owners didn't agree to pay the kidnappers. This must have been a tragedy for the owners and fans of Shergar. However, there may have been a happier ending. Of course, Shergar couldn't be alive today because this happened so many years ago. An optimist would say that he might not have been killed by the kidnappers. He could have died a natural death somewhere safe. We will probably never know.

▶ 10.02

Sally had worked as a trainee chef at a hotel for six months, but she was already dissatisfied with her job, especially the irregular hours and impolite customers. Also, Sally was still pretty inexperienced, but the head chef used to get impatient with her because she couldn't do everything. Sally started to lose her self-confidence. Did she have unreasonable expectations? Was she just another unsuccessful trainee, and would it be dishonest to continue at a job she couldn't do? It was highly improbable that things would get better. Sally got some informal advice from an old teacher, who told her to leave. For some reason – perhaps it meant she was irresponsible, too – Sally didn't listen to this advice, and she stayed at the hotel. This might seem incredible, but five years later, Sally is now head chef. She always smiles when her trainees tell her they want to leave.

▶ 10.03

1 The new parts are pretty inexpensive.
2 I find it improbable that they just happened to be in the same place at the same time.
3 The weather at this time of year is really unpredictable.
4 I won't go on a trip as disorganized as this one again.
5 I've dropped it on the floor a few times, but it's unbreakable.
6 I can do it, but it's kind of inconvenient, and I'm not very interested.

▶ 10.04

Shirley Chisholm (1924–2005) was the first African American woman elected to the U.S. Congress. In 1972, she became the first African American and the first woman to pursue the Democratic presidential nomination.
Chisholm was born in Brooklyn, New York. At Brooklyn College, she excelled on the debate team, and her professors encouraged her to go into politics. She started out teaching, but she stuck with her passion, joining organizations that tackled political and civil rights issues.
In 1968, she won a seat in the U.S. Congress. There "Fighting Shirley" tirelessly worked on civil rights issues. In 1972, she ran for president. She had to overcome plenty of racial discrimination; in fact, she was blocked from participating in the presidential debates, but she didn't give up – she took legal action and was allowed to give one televised speech. Although she lost the nomination, she continued in Congress until 1983. She coped with racism and sexism throughout her career, but "Fighting Shirley" will always be remembered as a woman who fought for change.

▶ 10.05

A Hi, Cleo. Thanks for coming to see me.

B No problem, Luke. What's up?

A Well, Diego has resigned.

B Hold on. I just talked to Diego yesterday. He didn't say anything.

A Well, it's true. One more thing. Diego's gone to Masons.

B But Masons is our competitor. That's a disaster!

A It's not a tragedy. We don't have any secrets he can tell them.

B That's true, I guess. Well, thanks for telling me. I'd better get back to work.

A Just a minute. There's something else we have to discuss. Would you be interested in taking Diego's job?

B What? I don't know about that. I'll have to think it over.

▶ 10.06

In the winter of 1855, the people of Devon in England woke up to find the footprints of a strange animal in the snow. Some frightened people followed them, and the footprints went on and on … for approximately a hundred miles – if their account is to be believed. The footprints went in a straight line through gardens and over walls and roofs. No one could explain the footprints, but since then many theories have been suggested. One of the strangest was that a kangaroo had escaped from a nearby zoo and jumped through the countryside!

▶ 10.07

JUAN I don't really know how I feel it went. I was really nervous before I went in and then, when I sat down, I saw there were three people on the other side of the table! That was kind of unexpected – I thought it would just be me and one other person. Anyway, I think it went pretty well – it was actually pretty informal, and they seemed to like me. There were a couple of questions I probably could have tackled better, but overall, I think my performance was really good.

MICHELLE I really don't know what happened. I couldn't have left it in the café because I had it with me when I bought the newspaper at the station. And then I guess I might have left it on the train somehow, but I don't remember taking it out of my pocket. It could have fallen out, I guess. If it did, I hope someone handed it in – it has everything inside – cards, driver's license, you know, all those kinds of things. But I have to admit, I don't feel very optimistic – there are so many dishonest people out there these days that you have to assume the worst, don't you?

GENO It was unbelievable, really – I was just walking past that clothing store and she stopped me, said hello, and started talking about how long it had been since we'd seen each other, all that kind of thing. But I had no idea who she was! She may have been someone I knew from school, or perhaps college, but I have a great memory for faces, and I just didn't recognize her. I think she must have confused me with someone else. Anyway, I didn't want to disappoint her, so I answered all her questions. Then we said goodbye and she walked away. It was really strange!

LIAM I think I'm very lucky. It all happened so quickly. One moment, I was going down the street, listening to my favorite podcast, and the next thing, there was a bang and the sound of glass breaking. I suppose I must have just lost control because of the rain – it was pouring at the time. In the end, there wasn't too much damage – there are a few repairs to do, but I can still drive it. And the wall I hit – well, that will have to be repaired too, and I think I'll have to pay for it. But I can't complain about that – I'm just glad I'm OK because I think I could have gotten really hurt.

EMILY Well, one moment, we were all just talking calmly and I was trying to get everyone to agree who would do what, and then suddenly he started shouting, saying I'm always trying to pass on my work to him and that I don't work hard enough. Aside from being untrue, it was also extremely unprofessional and very impolite, yelling like that in front of everyone. I'm really furious now – I mean, who does he think he is, behaving like that? It's not the first time he's lost his temper like that with someone, so it wasn't like a big surprise. I know he has a lot of problems, and I suppose he might have had a really bad day or something, but we're all under stress, aren't we? I'm going to have to file a formal complaint about him, I think.

ANSWER KEY

Unit 1

1A

1

a 2 has been 3 is he doing 4 was going 5 was talking 6 looks
7 invited 8 was making 9 Have you watched 10 dropped

c 2 Have, met 3 do, do 4 wrote 5 were coming 6 remember 7 didn't have
8 hasn't finished 9 are, getting 10 had produced

2

a 2 unsympathetic 3 inspiring 4 passionate 5 arrogant 6 motivated

b Across: 6 stubborn 8 optimistic
Down: 2 ambitious 3 determined 4 sensitive 5 respected 7 naive

3

a **Sound 1** /ɪ/: desire, prizes, revise
Sound 2 /e/: desert, helpful, identity, sensitive, slept
Sound 3 /ɜ/: dessert, prefer, service

1B

1

a 2 What did 3 Didn't 4 What for? 5 Which 6 weren't 7 that for
8 you could 9 if 10 Can 11 knows

c 2 Why is she going to do this?
3 Who doesn't need to register for the competition?
4 Why aren't they giving us our tickets?
5 Which of the challenges would you like to do?
6 What is the most difficult thing you have ever done?
7 What did we do all this hard training for?
8 What happened at the end of the game?
9 Do you think we have a chance of winning?
10 Who designed your website?

2

a 2 try out 3 give up 4 keep it up 5 manage to 6 stick with

b 2 drop out 3 stick with 4 work out 5 manage to 6 give up
7 keep it up 8 try out 9 make an effort

1C

1

a 2 c 3 b 4 a 5 c 6 b 7 b 8 c

2

a 4, 6, 2, 1, 5, 3

3

a Final /t/: 2, 5, 8, 9

1D

1

a True: 2, 5; False: 1, 3, 4, 6

b 2 b 3 b 4 c 5 a 6 c

2

a 2 Bad 3 Bad 4 Good 5 Good 6 Good 7 Good 8 Good

3

a Suggested answer
I live in a small town, but I use my car to get to work and go shopping because
it's easier. I walk short distances, usually when my husband has the car, but I
never bike, so naturally this was a new experience for me!

Both walking and biking are great exercise and surprisingly, I really enjoyed the
week because I saw lots of interesting things that I never usually notice. Quite
a few other people were walking and biking too, so it was really sociable. I also
saved a lot of money because gas is so expensive.

Inevitably, there were some problems. I needed more time to get to work, and
one day it rained, and that wasn't much fun on my bike. Unfortunately, biking
can be dangerous even in small towns because of all the traffic.

It was an interesting experience, but I think in modern life we do need to make
use of cars and public transportation because they are so convenient. We could
probably use them less, and this would be good for our health and the environment.

Reading and listening extension

1

a 3

b 2 a 3 b 4 c 5 b 6 a

2

a Reading down: 2, 3, 7, 1, 4, 5, 6

b 2 c 3 a 4 b 5 c 6 c 7 b 8 a

Review and extension

1

2 ✓
3 She's lived in that town since she was a child. / She has lived in that town since
she was a child.
4 Did you ever hear from her again afterward?
5 ✓
6 I don't know Tom. What's he like?
7 Why didn't you tell me?
8 ✓

2

2 Don't mention it to Laura. She's pretty sensitive about it.
3 The mayor is very respected in this town.
4 The president gave a passionate speech about crime.
5 ✓
6 ✓

3

2 b 3 c 4 e 5 d 6 g 7 f

Unit 2

2A

1

a 2 was speaking 3 had left 4 set 5 had been 6 were you doing 7 bought
8 had broken 9 were you waiting 10 gave

b 2 had finished 3 came 4 hadn't gone 5 burned / had burned
6 had started 7 had been crying 8 was getting 9 Did you see
10 had never been 11 went 12 was wearing 13 didn't get 14 ran

2

a 2 rid 3 hold 4 swept 5 point 6 attention 7 away 8 involved

b 2 get through 3 get the feeling 4 get anywhere 5 get into trouble
6 get on my nerves

3

"had": 2, 4, 6, 7, 9, 10

2B

1

a 2 unless 3 As long as 4 When 5 provided 6 In case 7 If 8 as long as
9 as soon as 10 If

c 2 c 3 h 4 a 5 f 6 d 7 g 8 e

72

a

A	E	N	V	I	R	O	N	M	E	N	T	E	U	L
K	N	C	R	H	B	E	X	U	D	D	O	X	K	E
X	D	T	S	G	T	I	C	U	L	E	T	C	E	L
S	A	D	S	N	P	C	L	N	Y	P	B	E	K	M
U	N	Q	E	T	B	S	R	I	A	R	N	P	Y	J
C	G	L	M	R	A	M	A	O	T	O	T	T	X	K
O	E	X	T	T	S	N	R	O	R	T	A	I	J	Z
C	R	E	A	T	U	R	E	Q	K	E	G	O	S	L
S	E	B	R	I	L	L	I	A	N	C	L	N	H	B
F	D	K	I	H	L	E	D	G	N	T	D	A	P	L
U	F	L	A	U	C	C	N	S	P	E	C	I	E	S
L	P	J	H	N	F	Y	Q	T	D	D	G	A	S	R
B	U	V	J	T	J	Z	Q	K	E	I	B	B	B	C
Y	Z	Z	I	I	R	M	P	H	A	B	I	T	A	T
S	K	T	S	X	A	Z	D	I	J	G	B	W	D	X

b 2 risk 3 extinct 4 survive 5 hunt 6 kill 7 environment 8 natural

2C

1

a 2 don't 3 did 4 wasn't 5 haven't 6 could 7 do 8 aren't

2

a 2 b 3 a 4 b 5 a 6 c

3

a Asking a question: 2, 5, 7, 10
Checking information: 3, 4, 6, 8, 9

2D

1

a 1 Getting Into the Sport

2 Training

3 What You Need

4 On the Day

b True: 1, 3, 4, 6, 8; False: 2, 5, 7

2

a c

3

a Suggested answer
Preparation
1 The best time to go is in the autumn. You can find more mushrooms in the morning, when there are fewer people around.
2 Mushrooms grow everywhere, but forests are the best place to find them. They grow near trees, so look carefully there.
3 It can be cool in a forest, so wear some warm clothes. You'll need good shoes or boots.
4 Check the weather forecast before you go.
In the forest
5 Be careful. There may be dangerous animals, but the biggest risk is simple accidents like falling.
6 You can't eat every mushroom. Go with someone experienced and never pick mushrooms you don't know. There are internet applications to check mushrooms.
7 Remember where you are going, use stones to mark your way if necessary. If you are lost, stay calm and plan how to get back.
8 Forests are beautiful places, so don't drop any litter or damage anything.
At home
9 Mushrooms don't last very long, so eat them at once or put them in the freezer.
10 There are many ways to cook mushrooms, for example, in soups and pies. Enjoy your tasty meal and start planning your next trip to the forest!

Reading and listening extension

1

a 1, 3, 5, 6

b 1 d 2 c 3 a 4 b

c True: 1, 3, 5, 7; False: 2, 4, 6, 8

a 2

b 2 a 3 b 4 c 5 b 6 a 7 c

Review and extension

1

2 ✓
3 I met Sarah three years ago, when I was a student.
4 She had been waiting for a chance, and she finally got one.
5 ✓
6 I'll watch it if it's on TV.

2

2 ✓
3 ✓
4 People could do more to protect the environment.
5 Every year, hundreds of animal species just disappear.
6 The Siberian tiger could soon become extinct.

3

2 face the fact 3 say it to my face 4 can't face 5 face a difficult choice 6 face the music

Unit 3

3A

1

a 2 down on 3 it out 4 into 5 on about 6 up 7 of 8 out 9 up to me
10 up

c 2 Try your hardest and don't let us down.
3 I fell out with Tony and we're not friends.
4 You can't get away with mistakes like that.
5 Go and figure it out for yourself.
6 Why don't you just try it out?
7 Michelle made it up to impress him.
8 You need to believe in what you're doing.
9 Can anyone come up with a better idea?
10 French is difficult, but I soon picked it up.

2

a 2 ability 3 outstanding 4 talent 5 successful 6 exceptional
7 potential 8 skilled

c 2 Olympic athletes are all exceptional in their field.
3 She's really successful at what she does.
4 I became very skilled at the game.
5 The ability to run long distances is important.
6 Work hard if you want to be extraordinary at a skill.
7 He has the potential to be world champion one day.
8 Carl Lewis was outstanding at the long jump.

3B

1

a 2 They won 3 did you think 4 haven't arrived 5 I was running
6 has been doing 7 completed 8 I've been running 9 played
10 been learning

b 2 ran 3 has beaten 4 held 5 has set 6 has also completed
7 has been running 8 has raced 9 has represented

2

a 2 referee 3 cheer 4 spectators 5 represent 6 field

b 2 compete 3 athletes 4 competitive 5 train 6 represent 7 victory
8 championships 9 records 10 cheer

3

a 2 compete 3 championships 4 professional 5 athlete
6 profession 7 training 8 performance 9 competitors
10 perform 11 victory 12 victorious

3C

a 2 Another thing to remember is the price.
3 I think maybe we should stay home.
4 Don't you think it's a good idea to ask?
5 How does it sound if we watch a movie on Sunday?
6 But don't you agree that it'd be easier to eat out?

b 2 Anyway, as I was saying, Tessa needs to decide.
3 Another idea might be to go the day before.
4 Just going back to what I was saying before.
5 I thought maybe we could invite Simon.
6 Of course, we could always check online.
7 But don't you agree that it'd be better to ask first? / But don't you agree that it would be better to ask first?
8 So, to get back to Martin and his problems.

a 2 beach V   peach U   7 pie U   buy V
3 ferry U   very V   8 pig V   pick U
4 simple U   symbol V   9 pack U   back V
5 girl V   curl U   10 have a V   have to U
6 save V   safe U

3D

1

a a3 b4 c5 e2

b 2 h 3 c 4 a 5 b 6 a

2

a 2 16 3 most 4 decrease 5 3 6 20

3

a Suggested answer

Sports are a very important part of life. Many people play sports, but they also enjoy following sports championships and events throughout the year. However, the number of loyal sports fans in the U.S. has decreased from Generation X to the Millennial generation.

The bar chart shows the number of loyal fans in five sports and compares those numbers between the two generations. The results show fans who closely follow each sport. You can see that every sport except basketball lost loyal followers. This is probably because of technology. Nowadays, sports fans have more options. They can follow more sports than ever before, and they don't have to watch complete games to see the best parts. Also, because of technology, people have shorter attention spans, so they prefer to watch highlights from different games and sports and to see more exciting moments in a shorter period.

There is a decrease in watching TV, perhaps because apps and social media provide instant access and news all the time. Also, millennials spend less time at home, so they prefer to use the Internet because it's more convenient for their lifestyles.

These results aren't surprising. They reflect the modern world where technology has changed so much of how we live. This trend may continue into the future as more people access different kinds of sports. They will probably follow more sports but less closely.

Review and listening extension

1

a 1, 2, 4

b 2 a 3 a 4 b 5 a 6 c 7 b 8 c

2

a 1 d 2 c 3 b 4 a 5 e

b 2 Tina 3 Mark 4 Mark 5 Mark 6 Both Mark and Tina

Review and extension

1

2 ✓
3 It's warm. Take your sweater off.
4 We're looking for a new secretary right now.
5 ✓
6 Monica hasn't been told about it yet.
7 Don't worry. I've already sent the letter.
8 I've been waiting for you for a long time!
9 ✓
10 I don't know. I haven't decided yet.

2

2 It's not possible to get there by public transportation.
3 No one doubts her ability to get to the very top.
4 It was another fantastic performance by the Kenyan.
5 ✓
6 ✓
7 What did the audience think of the movie?
8 The soccer players are just coming out on the field.

3

2 If you don't know it, look it up online.
3 She thought about it and decided not to bring the topic up. / She thought about it and decided not to bring up the topic.
4 I used it all up yesterday, so I went and bought some more.
5 We looked at the check and added it up again.
6 I went running with Percem, but I couldn't keep up with her.
7 I started to learn Spanish and picked it up pretty quickly.
8 He works so hard; I've always looked up to him.

Unit 4

4A

1

a 2 used to 3 wouldn't 4 lived 5 used to 6 wasn't 7 used to work
8 got used to 9 wasn't used to 10 get

b 2 graduated 3 used to 4 would sleep 5 realized 6 was used to
7 would go 8 decided 9 gotten used to 10 are used to visiting

2

a 2 No one knows what the effect was.
3 That's the main cause of the problem.
4 It could affect millions of people.
5 As a result of this, there is less money to spend.
6 The new law resulted in protests and demonstrations.
7 Generally, it's had a positive effect on people.

b 2 affect 3 result 4 is caused by 5 effect 6 as a result 7 lead

4B

1

a 2 I had to catch the 5:30 train.
3 No, I can work from home on Fridays.
4 Yes, the boss lets us stay at home one day.
5 Yes, I can find a seat on the train.
6 I'm tired during the day.
7 No, I don't have to unless we have a deadline.
8 You should speak to my boss!

b 2 ought to 3 doesn't have to 4 shoudn't 5 was supposed 6 don't need to
7 run 8 to eat 9 beat 10 forced to

2

a 2 rigorous 3 strict 4 exhausting 5 tough 6 tricky

b 2 rigorous 3 stretch 4 straightforward 5 arduous 6 tricky
7 challenge 8 demanding

3

a **Sound 1** /ʌ/: supper, result
Sound 2 /ʊ/: pull, sugar
Sound 3 /u/ or /ju/: useless, attitude, influential, enthusiasm

4C

1

a **Careful disagreement**
Really, do you think so?
Oh, I don't know.
Maybe you're right, but …
I know what you mean, but on the other hand …
I'm not sure about that.
Direct disagreement
That's just not true.
You can't really believe that.
No way!
I'm afraid you're wrong there.

b 2 I'm not sure about that. They work very hard.
3 Maybe you're right, but teachers are not the real problem.
4 Really, do you think so?
5 I know what you mean, but on the other hand, technology is so important.